HOW TO DRAW EVERYTHING FOR KIDS

300 STEP-BY-STEP DRAWINGS OF CUTE ANIMALS, VEHICLES, MONSTERS, ROBOTS, FOOD, GIFTS, AND MUCH MORE!

This book belongs to:

....

Special Art Learning

How to Draw Everything for Kids

300 Step-by-Step Drawings of Cute Animals,
Vehicles, Monsters, Robots, Food, Gifts, and Much More!

Published by Special Art Books
www.specialartbooks.com

Paperback ISBN: 9791255532613

Table of Contents

Animals

Vehicles & Machines

Fantasy & Adventure

Sports & Games

Sci-Fi & Space

Cool Objects & Fun Stuff

Food & Drinks

Holiday & Festive Characters

CHRISTMAS

HALLOWEEN

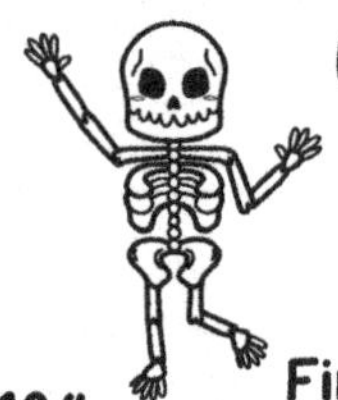

OTHER HOLIDAYS & FESTIVITIES

Introduction

Have you ever wanted to draw something cool but didn't know where to begin? Maybe you imagined a speeding race car, a hidden treasure map, or a fire-breathing dragon—but when you picked up your pencil, it felt too tricky to get it right.

Here's a secret: drawing awesome things isn't as hard as it looks! Every artist starts with simple shapes—circles, squares, and lines. When you connect them in just the right way, those shapes turn into alien spaceships, fearless superheroes, and other exciting creations!

In this book, you'll discover how to turn your imagination into amazing drawings, one easy step at a time. You'll build cool pictures from basic shapes, and before you know it, you'll have a collection of your own masterpieces to share, display, or gift to friends and family. Get ready to unleash your creativity, explore new adventures, and learn how to draw anything you can dream up!

How to Use this Book

You don't need a lot of tools when you practice drawing. You can use your favorite pencil and some of the crayons that you already have. Mistakes can happen, so remember to keep an eraser close by too! If you want to add some color to your artwork, consider these additional supplies:

When sketching with your pencil, draw gently to keep your lines clean and make corrections easy. Lightly trace and follow the arrows to complete your drawing. Afterwards, there's space for you to practice drawing on each activity page. Use the pages of this book as your drawing space and fill it up with your art—yes, you can even draw on the margins!

So what are you waiting for? Start drawing and have fun!

ANIMALS

Get wild with your pencil! From fierce creatures to awesome animals, you'll learn how to draw some of the coolest critters around.

LABRADOR RETRIEVER

It's your turn!

Don't be afraid to try new things, mix colors and have fun!

GERMAN SHEPHERD

It's your turn!

Don't be afraid to try new things, mix colors and have fun!

HUSKY

It's your turn!

Don't be afraid to try new things, mix colors and have fun!

PUG

It's your turn!

Don't be afraid to try new things, mix colors and have fun!

SIAMESE CAT

It's your turn!

Don't be afraid to try new things, mix colors and have fun!

PERSIAN CAT

It's your turn!

Don't be afraid to try new things, mix colors and have fun!

RABBIT

It's your turn!

Don't be afraid to try new things, mix colors and have fun!

GUINEA PIG

It's your turn!

Don't be afraid to try new things, mix colors and have fun!

HAMSTER

It's your turn!

Don't be afraid to try new things, mix colors and have fun!

GOLDFISH

It's your turn!

Don't be afraid to try new things, mix colors and have fun!

PARROT

It's your turn!

Don't be afraid to try new things, mix colors and have fun!

TURTLE

It's your turn!

Don't be afraid to try new things, mix colors and have fun!

CHAMELEON

It's your turn!

Don't be afraid to try new things, mix colors and have fun!

FROG

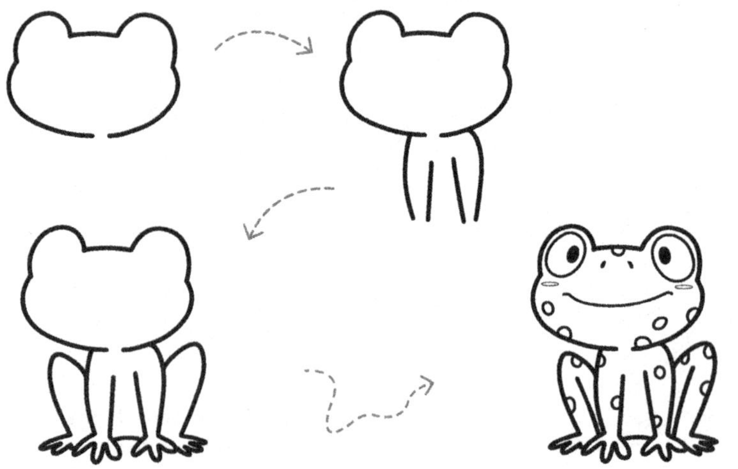

It's your turn!

Don't be afraid to try new things, mix colors and have fun!

SNAKE

It's your turn!

Don't be afraid to try new things, mix colors and have fun!

LION

It's your turn!

Don't be afraid to try new things,
mix colors and have fun!

TIGER

It's your turn!

Don't be afraid to try new things,
mix colors and have fun!

ELEPHANT

It's your turn!

Don't be afraid to try new things,
mix colors and have fun!

GIRAFFE

It's your turn!

Don't be afraid to try new things, mix colors and have fun!

GORILLA

It's your turn!

Don't be afraid to try new things, mix colors and have fun!

PANDA

It's your turn!

Don't be afraid to try new things, mix colors and have fun!

KANGAROO

It's your turn!

Don't be afraid to try new things, mix colors and have fun!

WOLF

It's your turn!

Don't be afraid to try new things, mix colors and have fun!

FOX

It's your turn!

Don't be afraid to try new things, mix colors and have fun!

DEER

It's your turn!

Don't be afraid to try new things,
mix colors and have fun!

BEAR

It's your turn!

Don't be afraid to try new things,
mix colors and have fun!

CHEETAH

It's your turn!

Don't be afraid to try new things,
mix colors and have fun!

BISON

It's your turn!

Don't be afraid to try new things, mix colors and have fun!

SQUIRREL

It's your turn!

Don't be afraid to try new things, mix colors and have fun!

EAGLE

It's your turn!

Don't be afraid to try new things, mix colors and have fun!

T-REX

It's your turn!

Don't be afraid to try new things, mix colors and have fun!

TRICERATOPS

It's your turn!

Don't be afraid to try new things, mix colors and have fun!

VELOCIRAPTOR

It's your turn!

Don't be afraid to try new things, mix colors and have fun!

BRACHIOSAURUS

It's your turn!

Don't be afraid to try new things, mix colors and have fun!

STEGOSAURUS

It's your turn!

Don't be afraid to try new things, mix colors and have fun!

SPINOSAURUS

It's your turn!

Don't be afraid to try new things, mix colors and have fun!

PTERODACTYL

It's your turn!

Don't be afraid to try new things, mix colors and have fun!

ANKYLOSAURUS

It's your turn!

Don't be afraid to try new things, mix colors and have fun!

MOSASAURUS

It's your turn!

Don't be afraid to try new things, mix colors and have fun!

DILOPHOSAURUS

It's your turn!

Don't be afraid to try new things, mix colors and have fun!

IGUANODON

It's your turn!

Don't be afraid to try new things, mix colors and have fun!

PARASAUROLOPHUS

It's your turn!

Don't be afraid to try new things, mix colors and have fun!

ALLOSAURUS

It's your turn!

Don't be afraid to try new things, mix colors and have fun!

MEGALODON

It's your turn!

Don't be afraid to try new things, mix colors and have fun!

SABERTOOTH TIGER

It's your turn!

Don't be afraid to try new things, mix colors and have fun!

SHARK

It's your turn!

Don't be afraid to try new things, mix colors and have fun!

WHALE

It's your turn!

Don't be afraid to try new things, mix colors and have fun!

DOLPHIN

It's your turn!

Don't be afraid to try new things, mix colors and have fun!

OCTOPUS

It's your turn!

Don't be afraid to try new things, mix colors and have fun!

STINGRAY

It's your turn!

Don't be afraid to try new things, mix colors and have fun!

JELLYFISH

It's your turn!

Don't be afraid to try new things, mix colors and have fun!

SEAHORSE

It's your turn!

Don't be afraid to try new things,
mix colors and have fun!

PIRANHA

It's your turn!

Don't be afraid to try new things,
mix colors and have fun!

CROCODILE

It's your turn!

Don't be afraid to try new things,
mix colors and have fun!

BALD EAGLE

It's your turn!

Don't be afraid to try new things, mix colors and have fun!

FALCON

It's your turn!

Don't be afraid to try new things, mix colors and have fun!

OWL

It's your turn!

Don't be afraid to try new things, mix colors and have fun!

HAWK

It's your turn!

Don't be afraid to try new things, mix colors and have fun!

PHOENIX

It's your turn!

Don't be afraid to try new things, mix colors and have fun!

GRIFFIN

It's your turn!

Don't be afraid to try new things, mix colors and have fun!

VEHICLES and MACHINES

Rev up those engines! In this chapter, you'll draw speedy cars, flying planes, powerful trucks, and awesome machines built for action.

SPORTS CAR

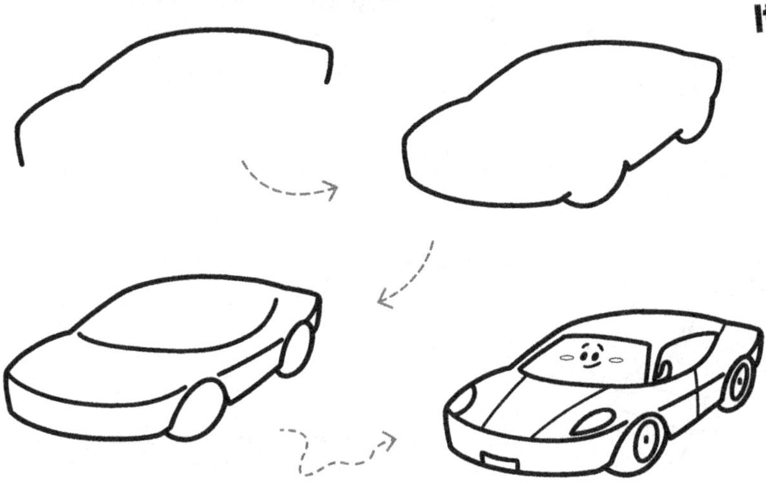

It's your turn!

Don't be afraid to try new things,
mix colors and have fun!

MONSTER TRUCK

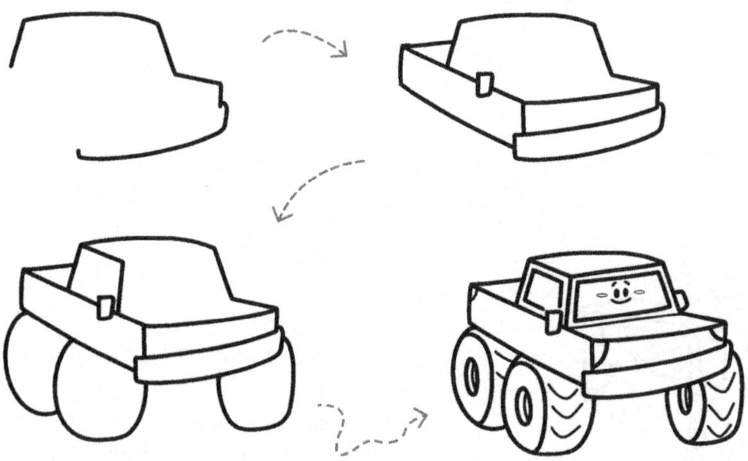

It's your turn!

Don't be afraid to try new things,
mix colors and have fun!

FORMULA 1 CAR

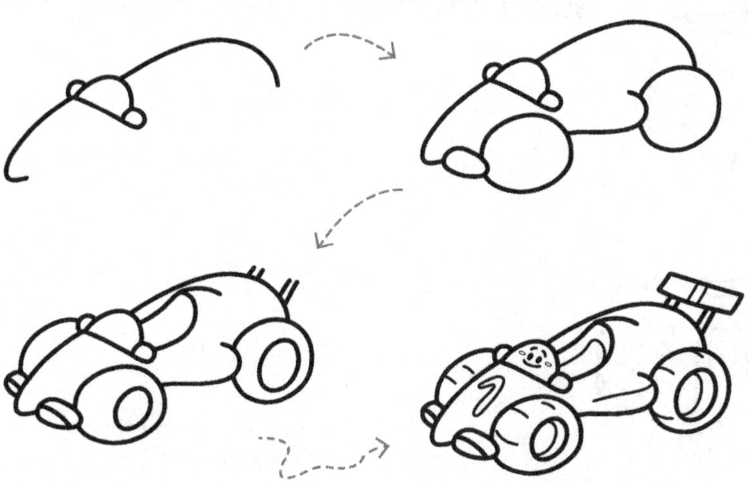

It's your turn!

Don't be afraid to try new things,
mix colors and have fun!

POLICE CAR

It's your turn!

Don't be afraid to try new things, mix colors and have fun!

FIRE TRUCK

It's your turn!

Don't be afraid to try new things, mix colors and have fun!

AMBULANCE

It's your turn!

Don't be afraid to try new things, mix colors and have fun!

TRACTOR

It's your turn!

Don't be afraid to try new things, mix colors and have fun!

TANK

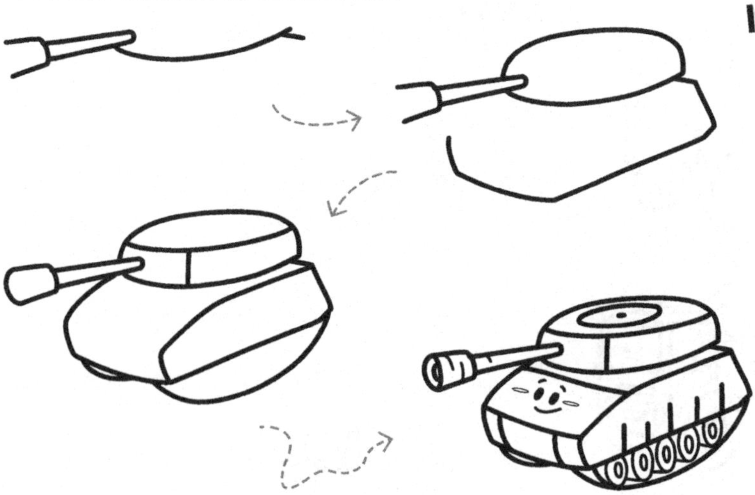

It's your turn!

Don't be afraid to try new things, mix colors and have fun!

OFF-ROAD JEEP

It's your turn!

Don't be afraid to try new things, mix colors and have fun!

EXCAVATOR

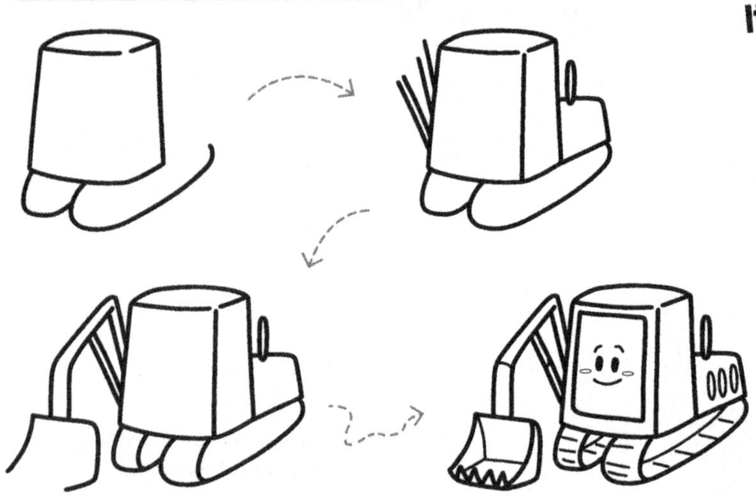

It's your turn!

Don't be afraid to try new things, mix colors and have fun!

CEMENT MIXER

It's your turn!

Don't be afraid to try new things, mix colors and have fun!

DUMP TRUCK

It's your turn!

Don't be afraid to try new things, mix colors and have fun!

SCHOOL BUS

It's your turn!

Don't be afraid to try new things, mix colors and have fun!

RALLY CAR

It's your turn!

Don't be afraid to try new things, mix colors and have fun!

GARBAGE TRUCK

It's your turn!

Don't be afraid to try new things, mix colors and have fun!

MOTORCYCLE

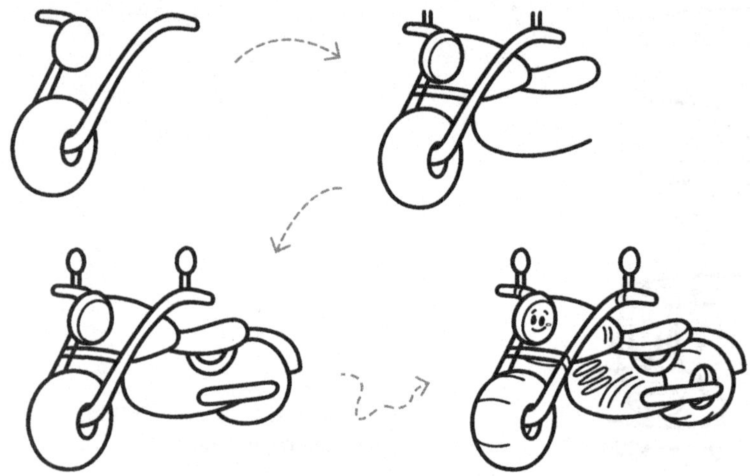

It's your turn!

Don't be afraid to try new things, mix colors and have fun!

SCOOTER

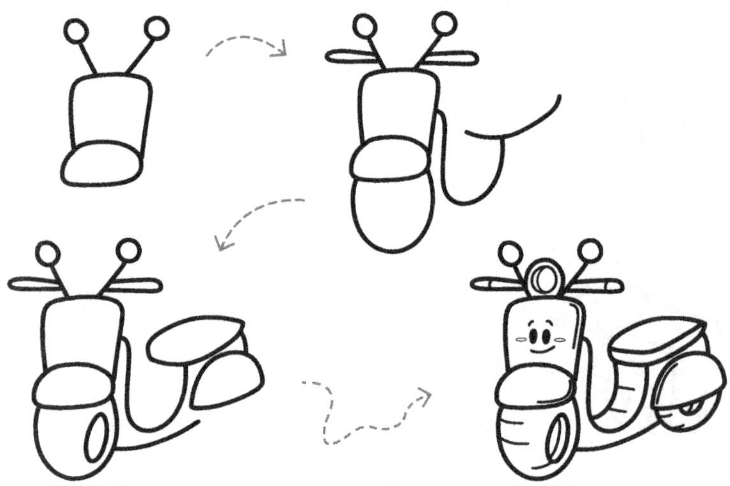

It's your turn!

Don't be afraid to try new things, mix colors and have fun!

QUAD BIKE

It's your turn!

Don't be afraid to try new things, mix colors and have fun!

SKATEBOARD

It's your turn!

Don't be afraid to try new things, mix colors and have fun!

BICYCLE

It's your turn!

Don't be afraid to try new things, mix colors and have fun!

JET FIGHTER

It's your turn!

Don't be afraid to try new things, mix colors and have fun!

COMMERCIAL AIRPLANE

It's your turn!

Don't be afraid to try new things, mix colors and have fun!

HELICOPTER

It's your turn!

Don't be afraid to try new things, mix colors and have fun!

BIPLANE

It's your turn!

Don't be afraid to try new things, mix colors and have fun!

HOT AIR BALLOON

It's your turn!

Don't be afraid to try new things, mix colors and have fun!

BLIMP

It's your turn!

Don't be afraid to try new things, mix colors and have fun!

SPACE SHUTTLE

It's your turn!

Don't be afraid to try new things, mix colors and have fun!

ROCKET

It's your turn!

Don't be afraid to try new things, mix colors and have fun!

UFO

It's your turn!

Don't be afraid to try new things, mix colors and have fun!

SPACESHIP

It's your turn!

Don't be afraid to try new things, mix colors and have fun!

SATELLITE

It's your turn!

Don't be afraid to try new things, mix colors and have fun!

MARS ROVER

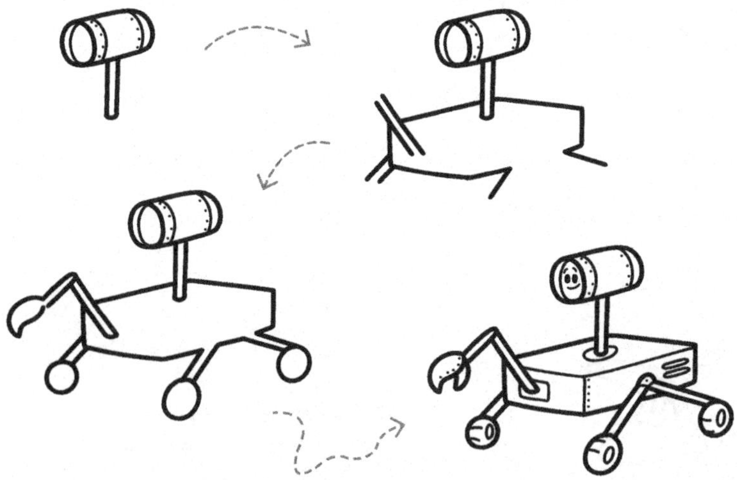

It's your turn!

Don't be afraid to try new things, mix colors and have fun!

ASTEROID MINER

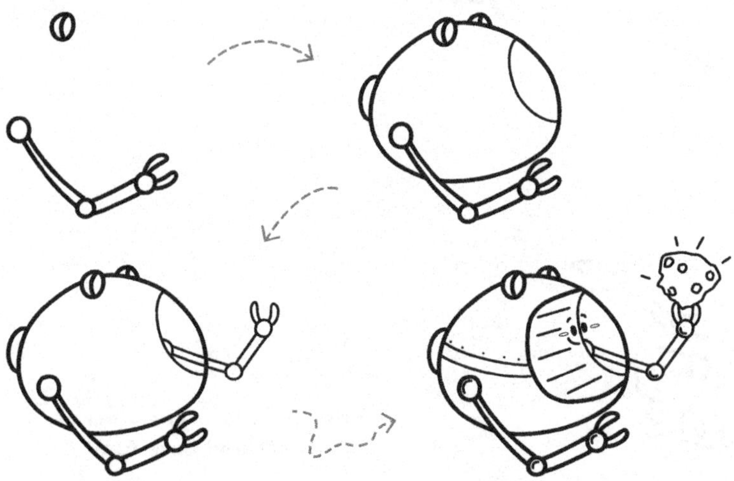

It's your turn!

Don't be afraid to try new things, mix colors and have fun!

FLYING CAR

It's your turn!

Don't be afraid to try new things, mix colors and have fun!

STEALTH BOMBER

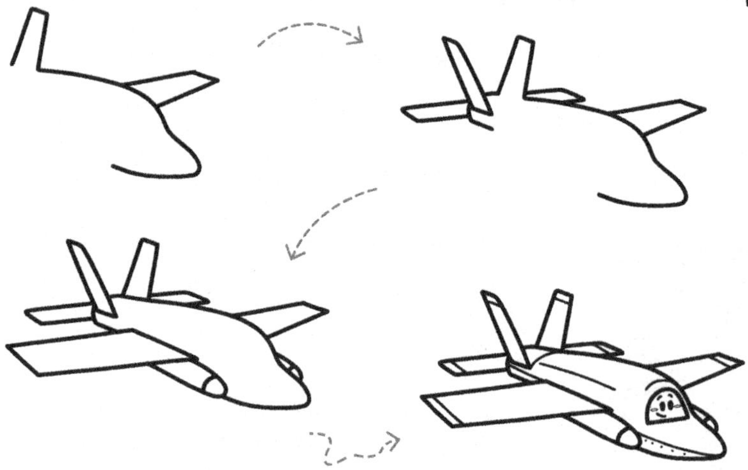

It's your turn!

Don't be afraid to try new things, mix colors and have fun!

DRONE

It's your turn!

Don't be afraid to try new things, mix colors and have fun!

PARAGLIDER WING

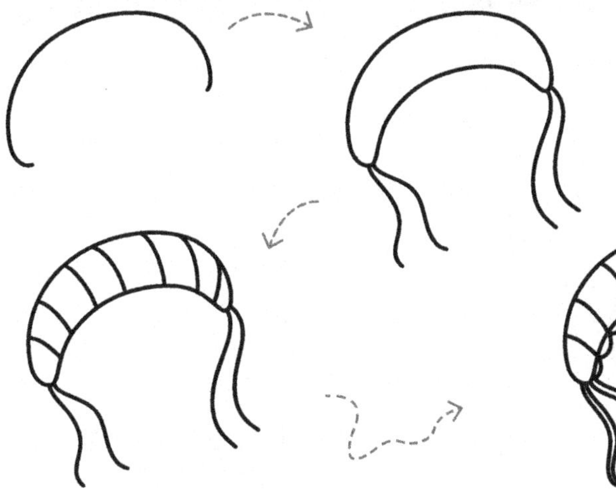

It's your turn!

Don't be afraid to try new things, mix colors and have fun!

JETPACK

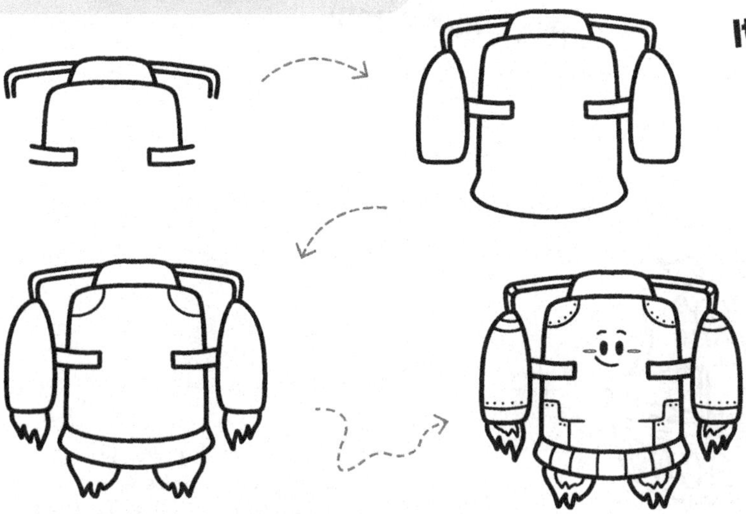

It's your turn!

Don't be afraid to try new things, mix colors and have fun!

JELLY ALIEN

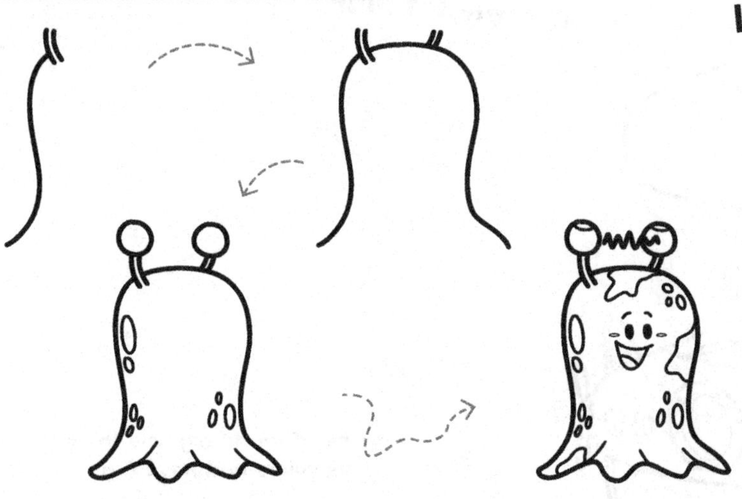

It's your turn!

Don't be afraid to try new things, mix colors and have fun!

HOVERCRAFT

It's your turn!

Don't be afraid to try new things, mix colors and have fun!

PIRATE SHIP

It's your turn!

Don't be afraid to try new things, mix colors and have fun!

SUBMARINE

It's your turn!

Don't be afraid to try new things, mix colors and have fun!

SPEEDBOAT

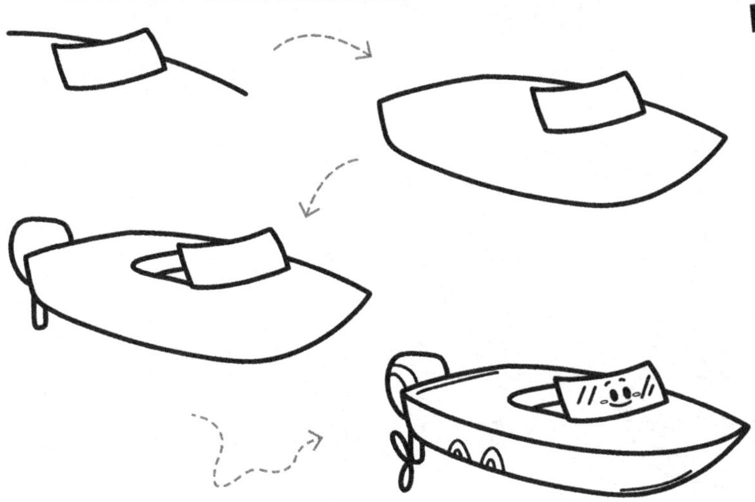

It's your turn!

Don't be afraid to try new things, mix colors and have fun!

CRUISE SHIP

It's your turn!

Don't be afraid to try new things, mix colors and have fun!

FISHING BOAT

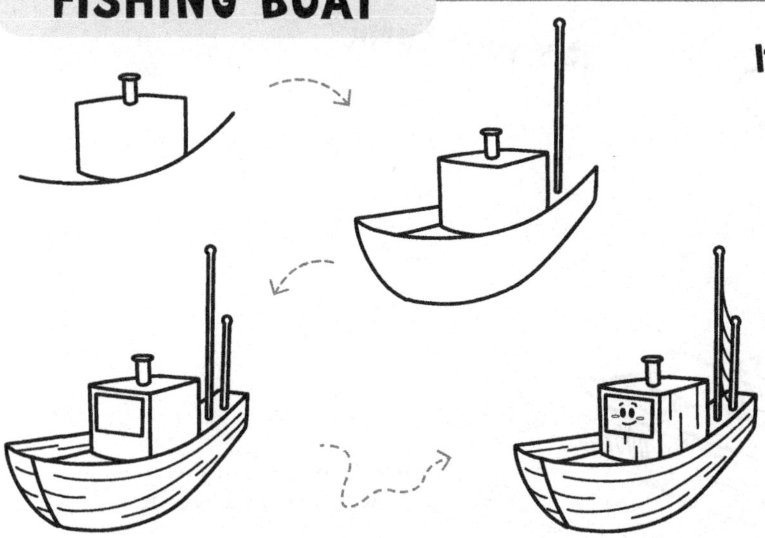

It's your turn!

Don't be afraid to try new things, mix colors and have fun!

VIKING SHIP

It's your turn!

Don't be afraid to try new things, mix colors and have fun!

AIRCRAFT CARRIER

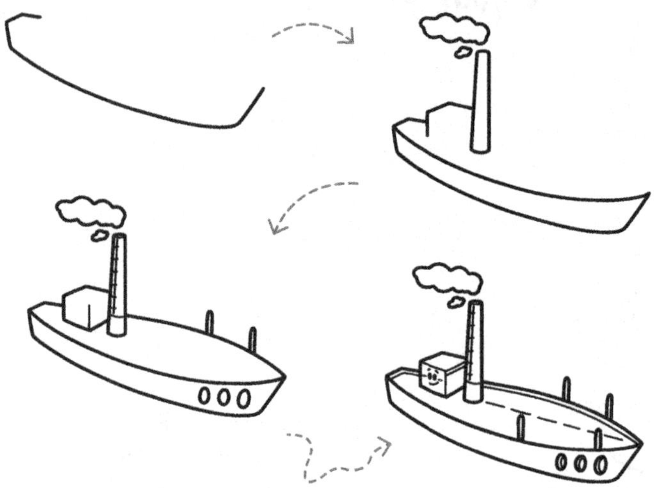

It's your turn!

Don't be afraid to try new things, mix colors and have fun!

JET SKI

It's your turn!

Don't be afraid to try new things, mix colors and have fun!

RAFT

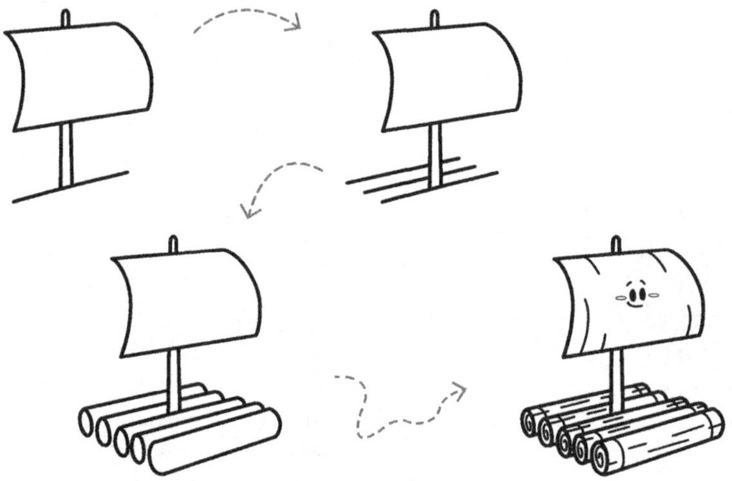

It's your turn!

Don't be afraid to try new things,
mix colors and have fun!

SURFBOARD

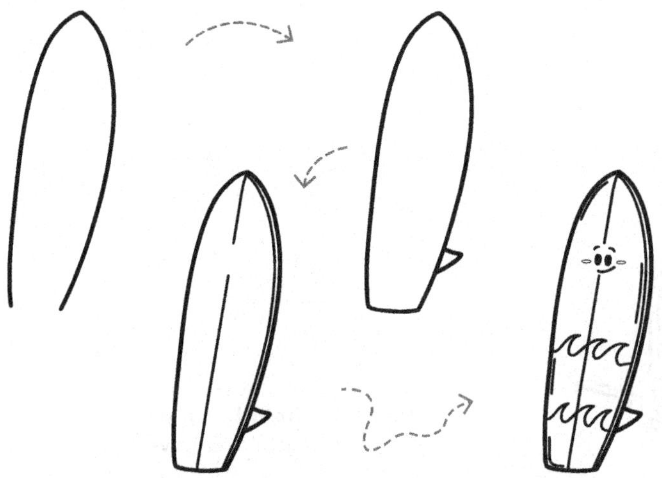

It's your turn!

Don't be afraid to try new things,
mix colors and have fun!

HOVERBIKE

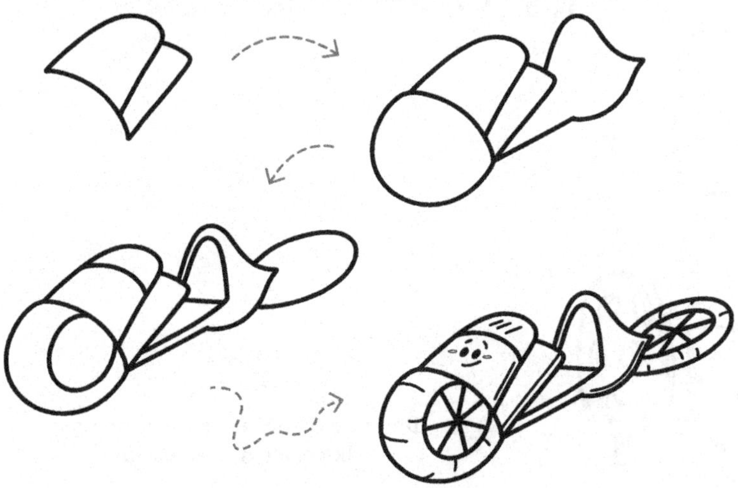

It's your turn!

Don't be afraid to try new things,
mix colors and have fun!

MECH ROBOT

It's your turn!

Don't be afraid to try new things, mix colors and have fun!

FLYING TRAIN

It's your turn!

Don't be afraid to try new things, mix colors and have fun!

UNDERWATER BASE

It's your turn!

Don't be afraid to try new things, mix colors and have fun!

SPACESHIP RACER

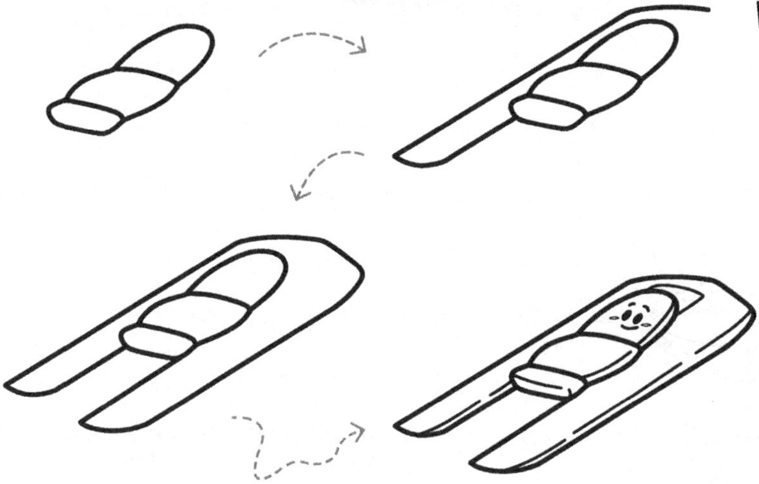

It's your turn!

Don't be afraid to try new things,
mix colors and have fun!

CYBER TRUCK

It's your turn!

Don't be afraid to try new things,
mix colors and have fun!

ALIEN HOVERPOD

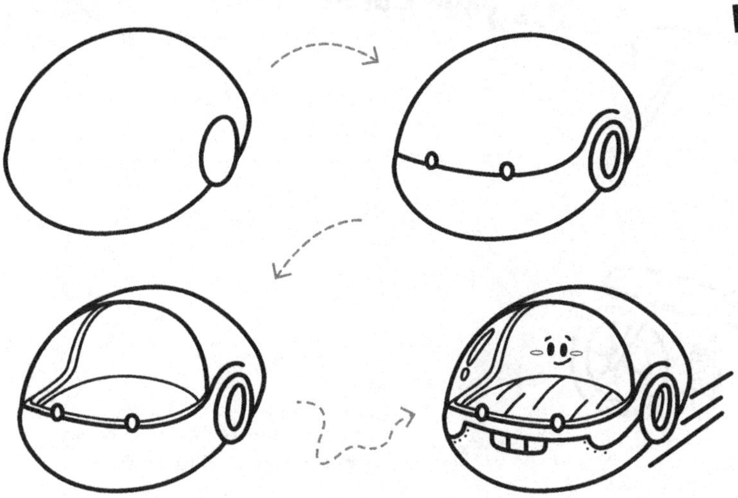

It's your turn!

Don't be afraid to try new things,
mix colors and have fun!

STEAMPUNK ZEPPELIN

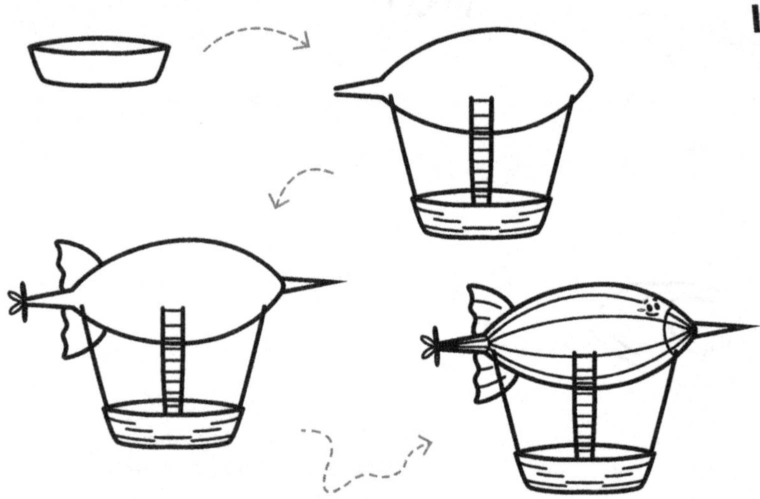

It's your turn!

Don't be afraid to try new things, mix colors and have fun!

TIME MACHINE

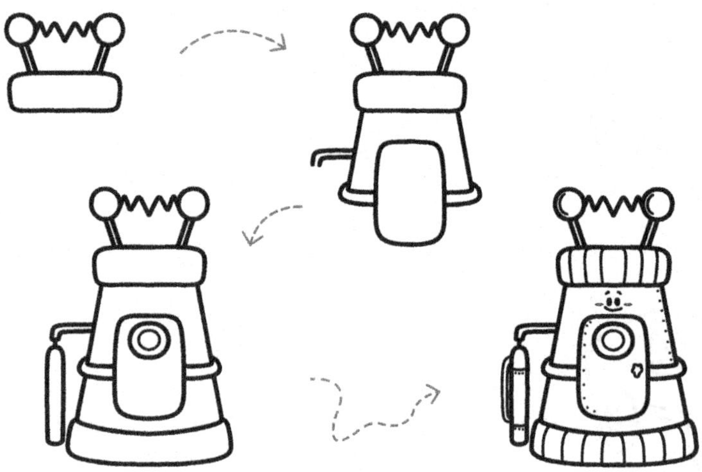

It's your turn!

Don't be afraid to try new things, mix colors and have fun!

SPACE MOTORCYCLE

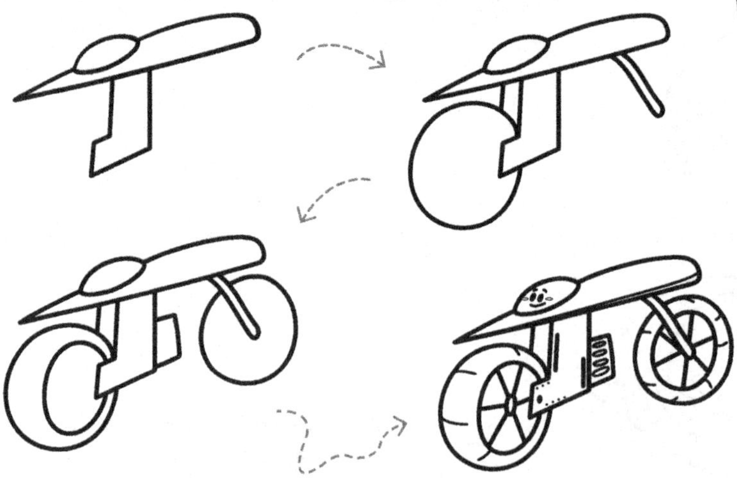

It's your turn!

Don't be afraid to try new things, mix colors and have fun!

FANTASY and ADVENTURE

Step into an epic world of magic and danger! Draw daring heroes, wild monsters, and legendary creatures ready for adventure.

SUPERHERO

It's your turn!

Don't be afraid to try new things, mix colors and have fun!

NINJA

It's your turn!

Don't be afraid to try new things, mix colors and have fun!

KNIGHT

It's your turn!

Don't be afraid to try new things, mix colors and have fun!

SAMURAI

It's your turn!

Don't be afraid to try new things,
mix colors and have fun!

PIRATE

It's your turn!

Don't be afraid to try new things,
mix colors and have fun!

SPY

It's your turn!

Don't be afraid to try new things,
mix colors and have fun!

SECRET AGENT

It's your turn!

Don't be afraid to try new things, mix colors and have fun!

SPACE EXPLORER

It's your turn!

Don't be afraid to try new things, mix colors and have fun!

COWBOY

It's your turn!

Don't be afraid to try new things, mix colors and have fun!

VIKING

It's your turn!

Don't be afraid to try new things, mix colors and have fun!

ROUND ROBOT

It's your turn!

Don't be afraid to try new things, mix colors and have fun!

CYBORG

It's your turn!

Don't be afraid to try new things, mix colors and have fun!

MARTIAL ARTIST

It's your turn!

Don't be afraid to try new things, mix colors and have fun!

GLADIATOR

It's your turn!

Don't be afraid to try new things, mix colors and have fun!

ALIEN WARRIOR

It's your turn!

Don't be afraid to try new things, mix colors and have fun!

GIANT ROBOT

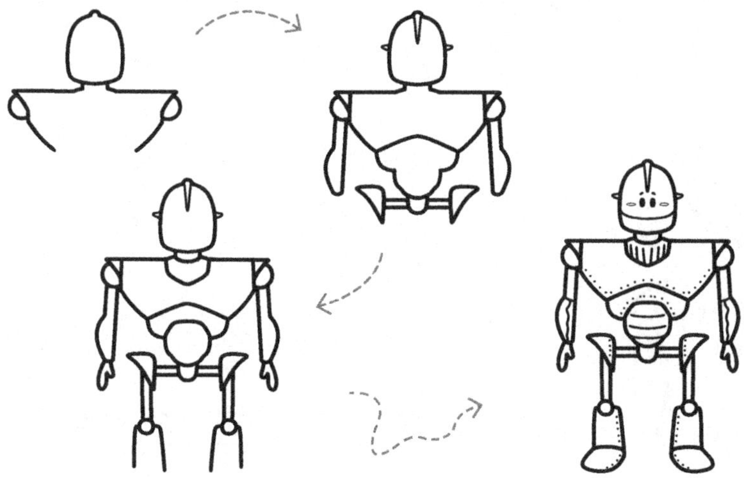

It's your turn!

Don't be afraid to try new things, mix colors and have fun!

ROBOT FIGHTER

It's your turn!

Don't be afraid to try new things, mix colors and have fun!

DEMON SLAYER

It's your turn!

Don't be afraid to try new things, mix colors and have fun!

WIZARD WARRIOR

It's your turn!

Don't be afraid to try new things,
mix colors and have fun!

ZOMBIE HUNTER

It's your turn!

Don't be afraid to try new things,
mix colors and have fun!

FIRE-BREATHING DRAGON

It's your turn!

Don't be afraid to try new things,
mix colors and have fun!

ICE DRAGON

It's your turn!

Don't be afraid to try new things,
mix colors and have fun!

WEREWOLF

It's your turn!

Don't be afraid to try new things,
mix colors and have fun!

MINOTAUR

It's your turn!

Don't be afraid to try new things,
mix colors and have fun!

CYCLOPS

It's your turn!

Don't be afraid to try new things, mix colors and have fun!

KRAKEN

It's your turn!

Don't be afraid to try new things, mix colors and have fun!

GHOST

It's your turn!

Don't be afraid to try new things, mix colors and have fun!

MUMMY

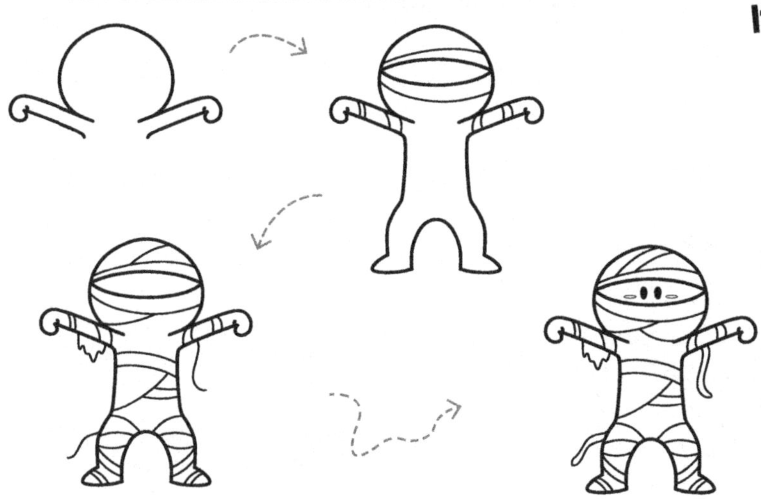

It's your turn!

Don't be afraid to try new things, mix colors and have fun!

GOBLIN

It's your turn!

Don't be afraid to try new things, mix colors and have fun!

SEA MONSTER

It's your turn!

Don't be afraid to try new things, mix colors and have fun!

YETI

It's your turn!

Don't be afraid to try new things,
mix colors and have fun!

LOCH NESS MONSTER

It's your turn!

Don't be afraid to try new things,
mix colors and have fun!

THREE-HEADED MONSTER

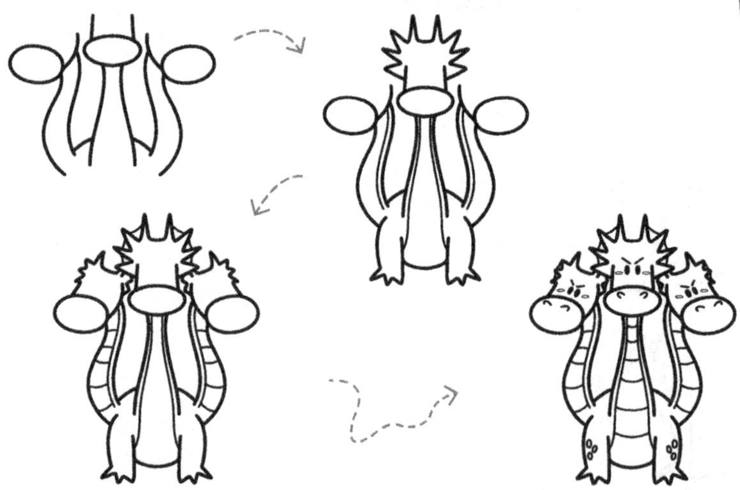

It's your turn!

Don't be afraid to try new things,
mix colors and have fun!

SHADOW DEMON

It's your turn!

Don't be afraid to try new things, mix colors and have fun!

OGRE

It's your turn!

Don't be afraid to try new things, mix colors and have fun!

SACI PERERE

It's your turn!

Don't be afraid to try new things, mix colors and have fun!

EVIL CLOWN

It's your turn!

Don't be afraid to try new things, mix colors and have fun!

ROBOT MONSTER

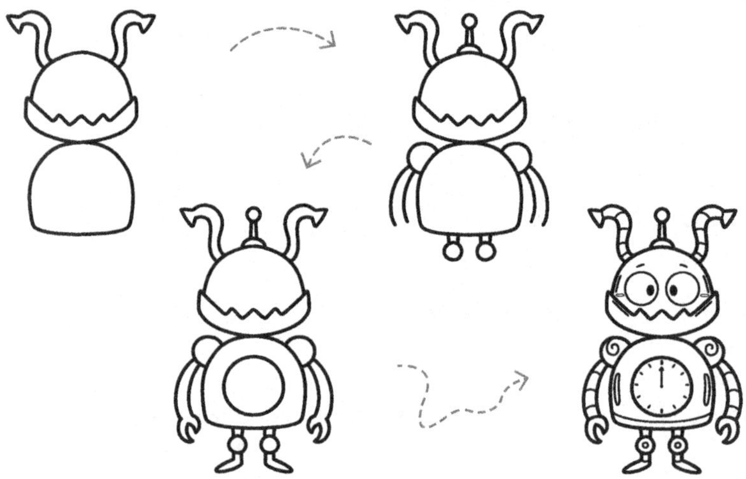

It's your turn!

Don't be afraid to try new things, mix colors and have fun!

SKELETON WARRIOR

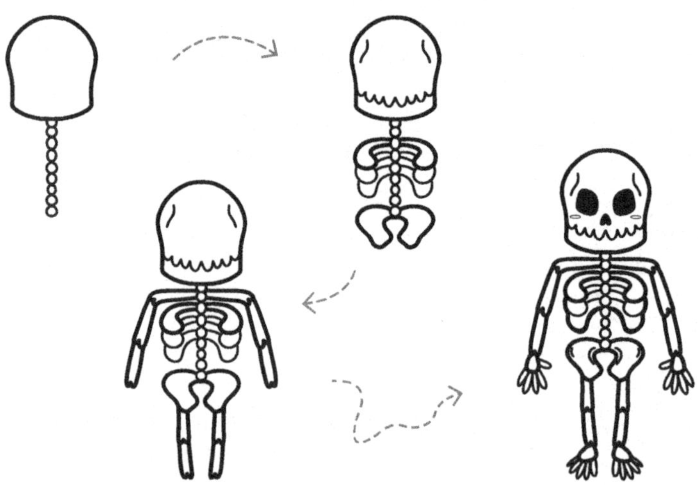

It's your turn!

Don't be afraid to try new things, mix colors and have fun!

MUTANT CREATURE

It's your turn!

Don't be afraid to try new things, mix colors and have fun!

SWORD

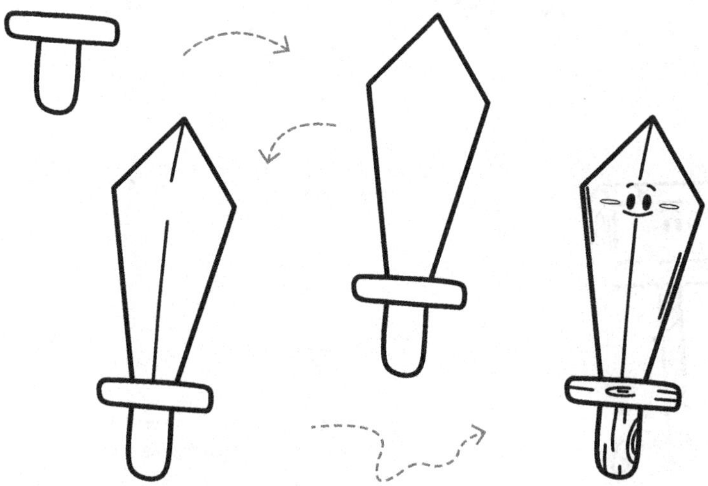

It's your turn!

Don't be afraid to try new things, mix colors and have fun!

KATANA

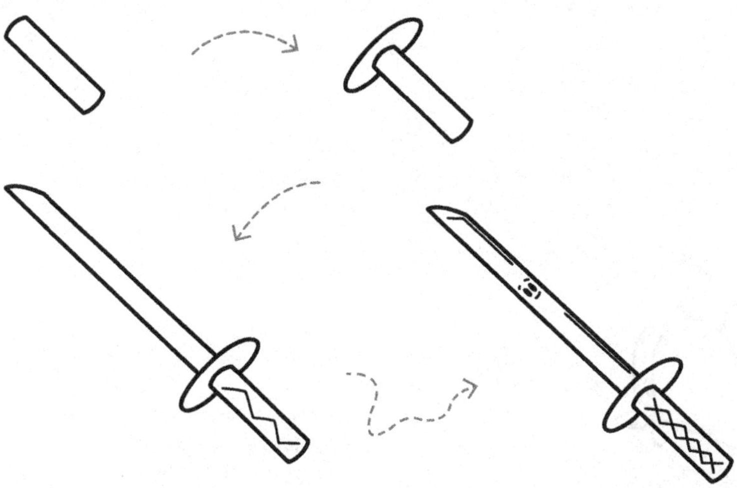

It's your turn!

Don't be afraid to try new things, mix colors and have fun!

VIKING AXE

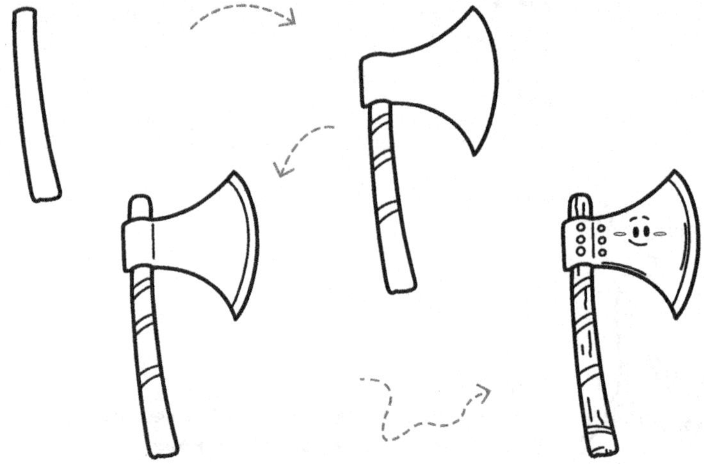

It's your turn!

Don't be afraid to try new things, mix colors and have fun!

WAR HAMMER

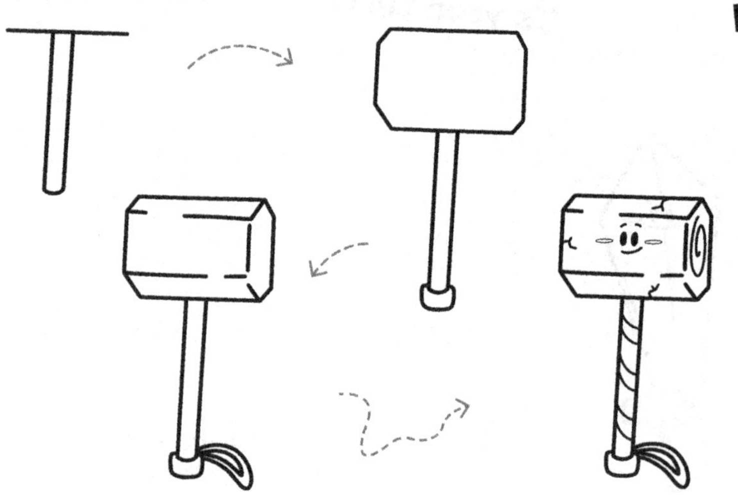

It's your turn!

Don't be afraid to try new things, mix colors and have fun!

BOW & ARROW

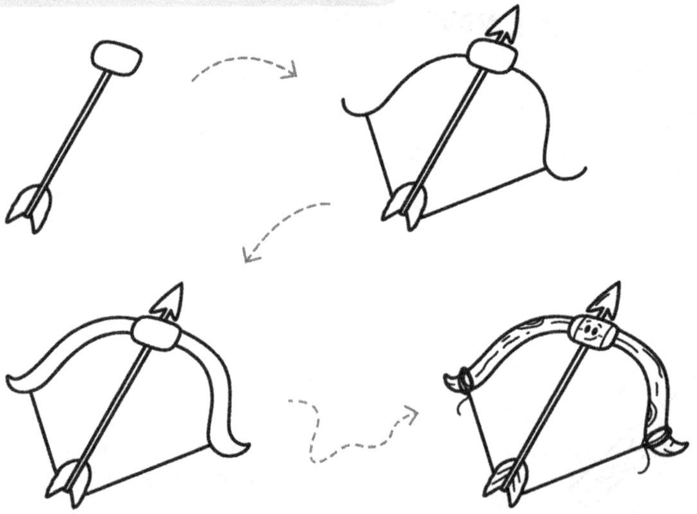

It's your turn!

Don't be afraid to try new things, mix colors and have fun!

LASER GUN

It's your turn!

Don't be afraid to try new things, mix colors and have fun!

SCI-FI SHIELD

It's your turn!

Don't be afraid to try new things, mix colors and have fun!

ALIEN BLASTER

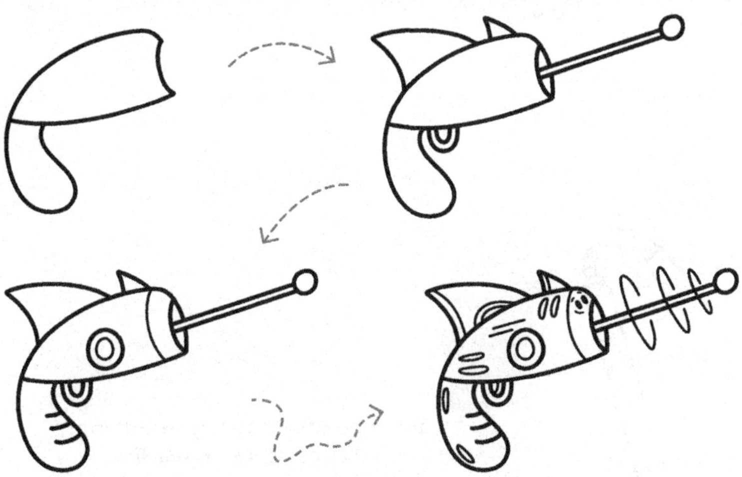

It's your turn!

Don't be afraid to try new things, mix colors and have fun!

LIGHTSABER

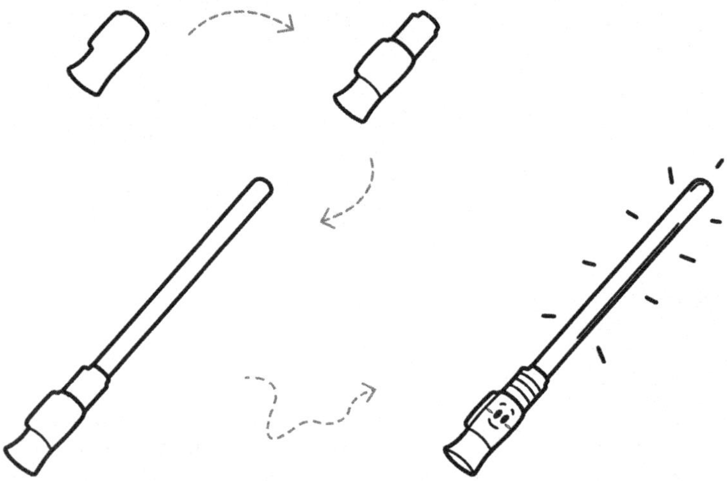

It's your turn!

Don't be afraid to try new things, mix colors and have fun!

MAGICAL WAND

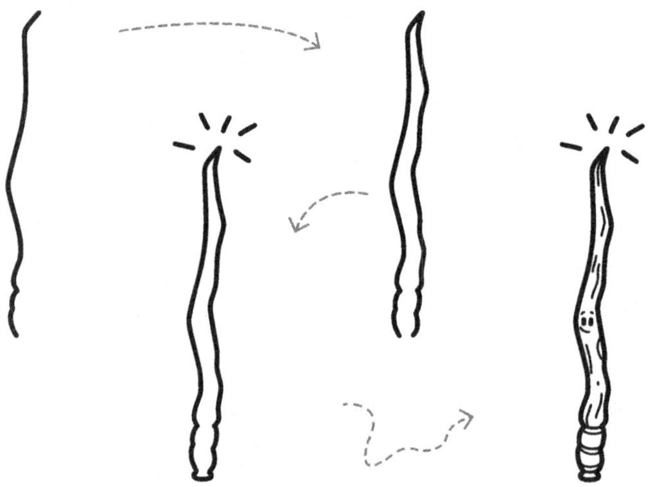

It's your turn!

Don't be afraid to try new things, mix colors and have fun!

NUNCHUCKS

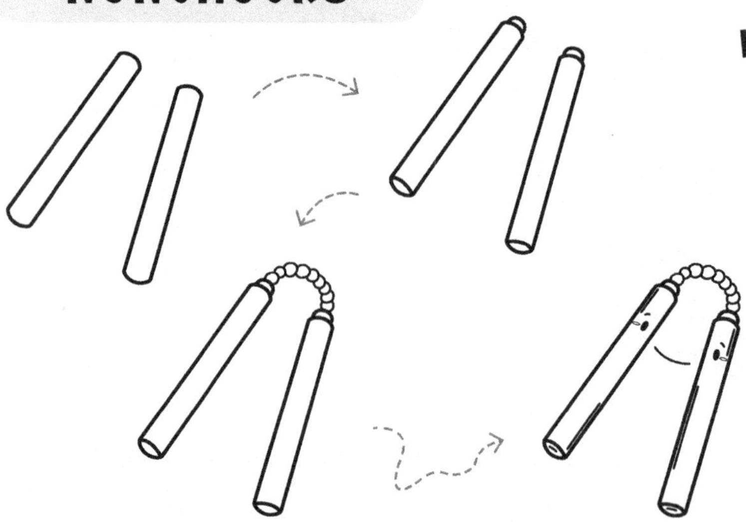

It's your turn!

Don't be afraid to try new things, mix colors and have fun!

BOOMERANG

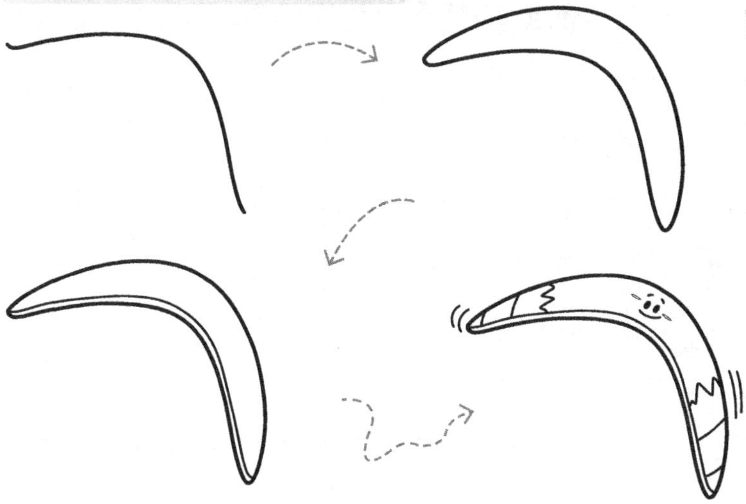

It's your turn!

Don't be afraid to try new things, mix colors and have fun!

CROSSBOW

It's your turn!

Don't be afraid to try new things, mix colors and have fun!

ELECTRIC WHIP

It's your turn!

Don't be afraid to try new things, mix colors and have fun!

TELESCOPE

It's your turn!

Don't be afraid to try new things, mix colors and have fun!

STEAMPUNK GUN

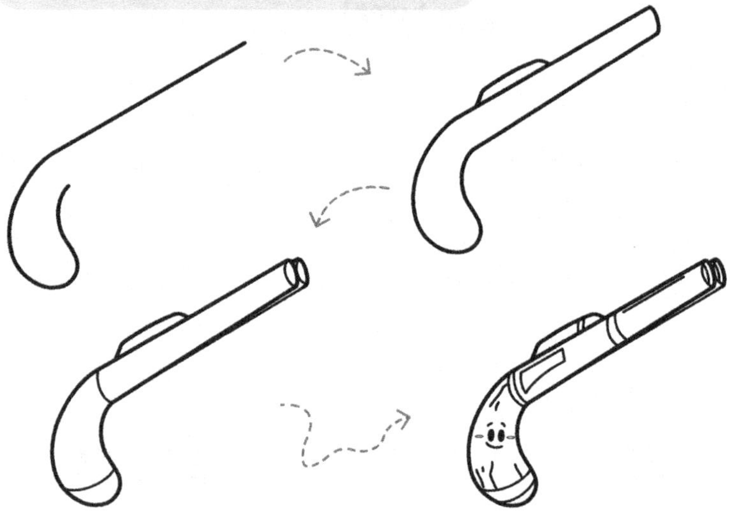

It's your turn!

Don't be afraid to try new things, mix colors and have fun!

ENERGY GAUNTLET

It's your turn!

Don't be afraid to try new things, mix colors and have fun!

GRAPPLING HOOK

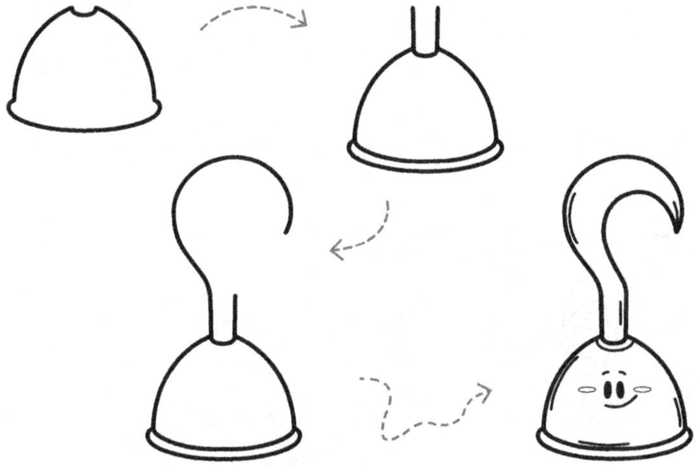

It's your turn!

Don't be afraid to try new things, mix colors and have fun!

ROUND AIRCRAFT

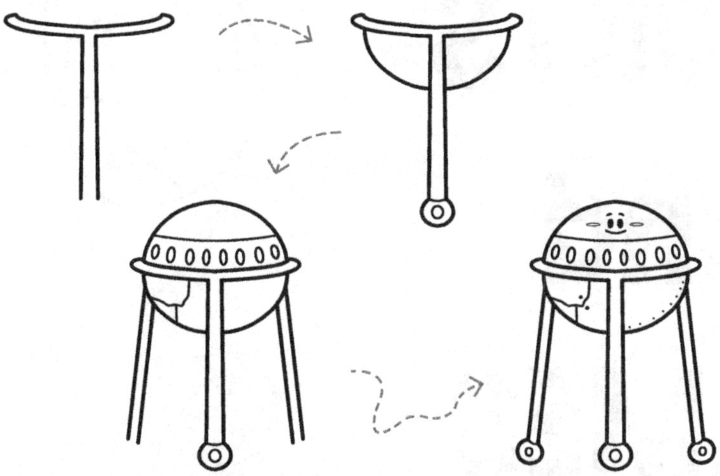

It's your turn!

Don't be afraid to try new things, mix colors and have fun!

SECRET AGENT WATCH

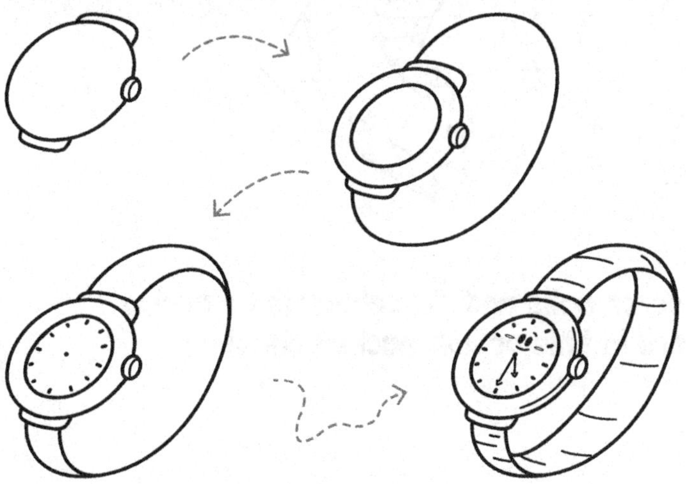

It's your turn!

Don't be afraid to try new things, mix colors and have fun!

SPORTS and GAMES

Game on! Draw everything from soccer balls and skateboards to racing bikes and video game controllers in this action-packed chapter

SOCCER BALL

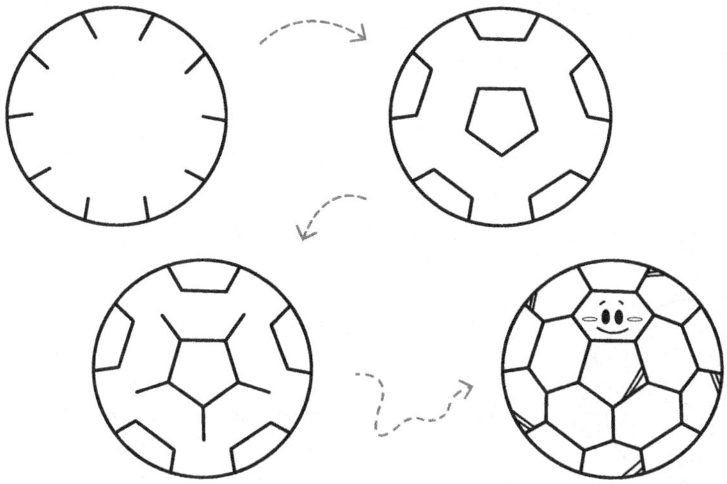

It's your turn!

Don't be afraid to try new things, mix colors and have fun!

BASKETBALL

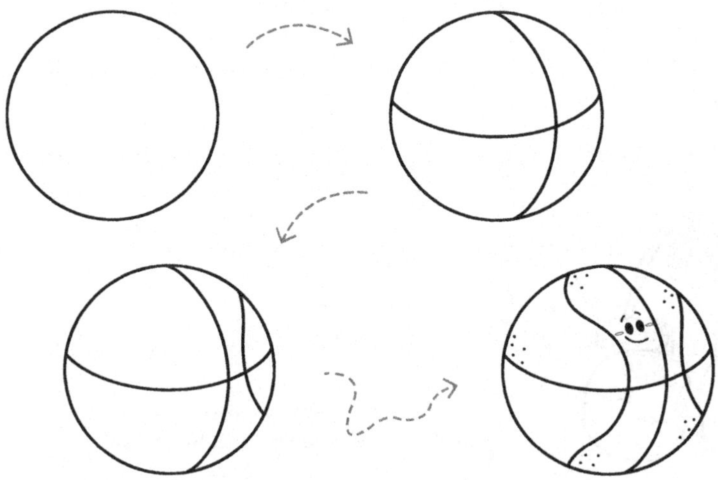

It's your turn!

Don't be afraid to try new things, mix colors and have fun!

BASEBALL

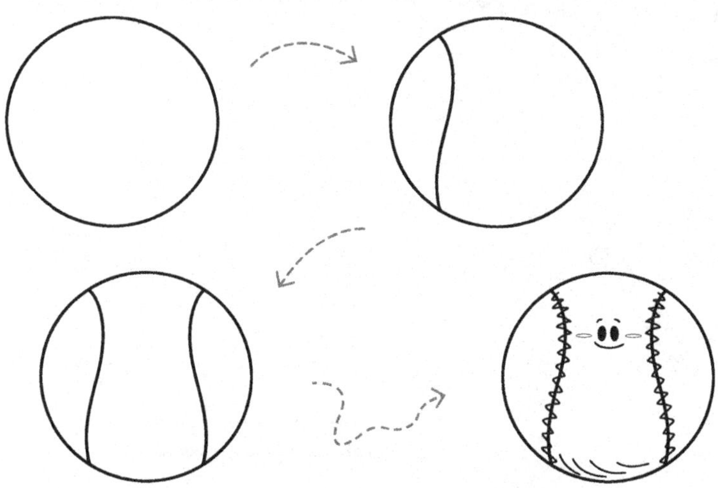

It's your turn!

Don't be afraid to try new things, mix colors and have fun!

FOOTBALL HELMET

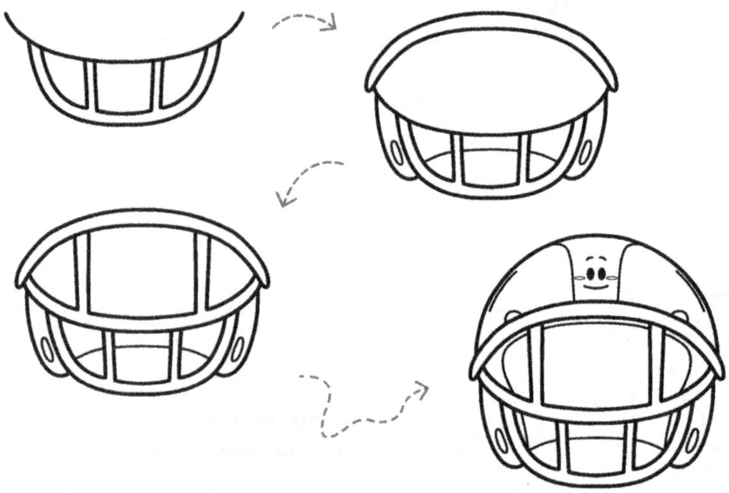

It's your turn!

Don't be afraid to try new things, mix colors and have fun!

BOXING GLOVES

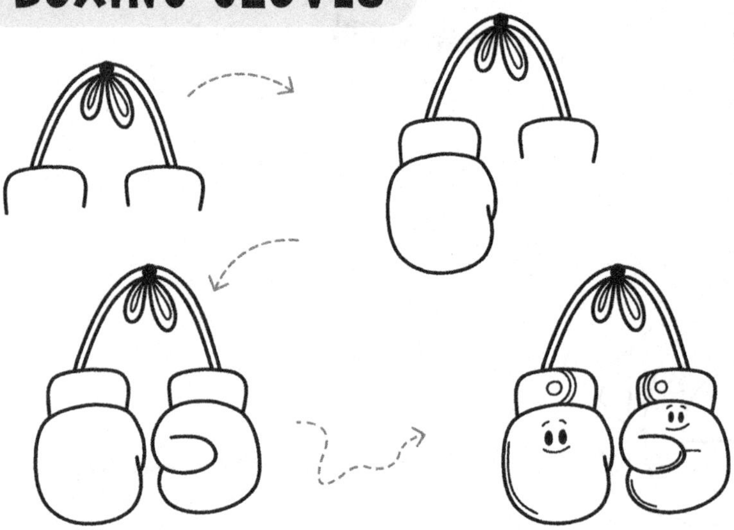

It's your turn!

Don't be afraid to try new things, mix colors and have fun!

HOCKEY STICK

It's your turn!

Don't be afraid to try new things, mix colors and have fun!

ICE SKATES

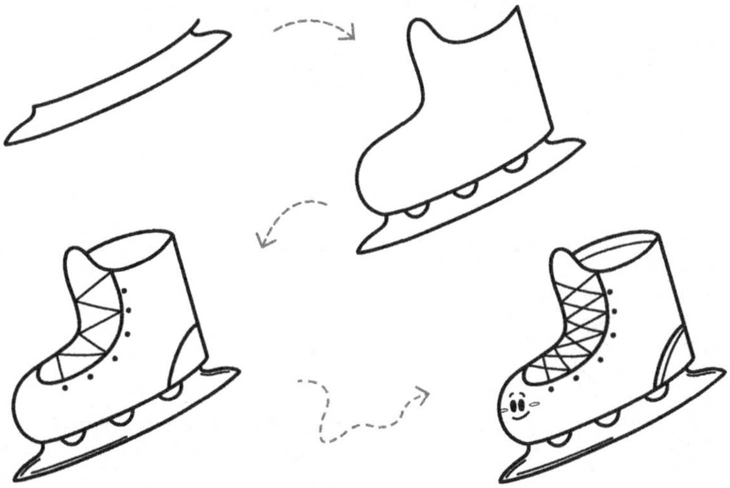

It's your turn!

Don't be afraid to try new things, mix colors and have fun!

BASEBALL BAT

It's your turn!

Don't be afraid to try new things, mix colors and have fun!

SNORKEL MASK

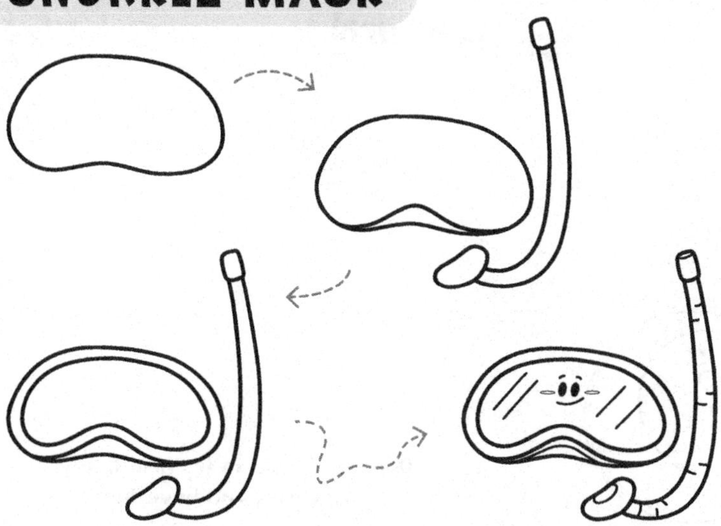

It's your turn!

Don't be afraid to try new things, mix colors and have fun!

FOOTBALL

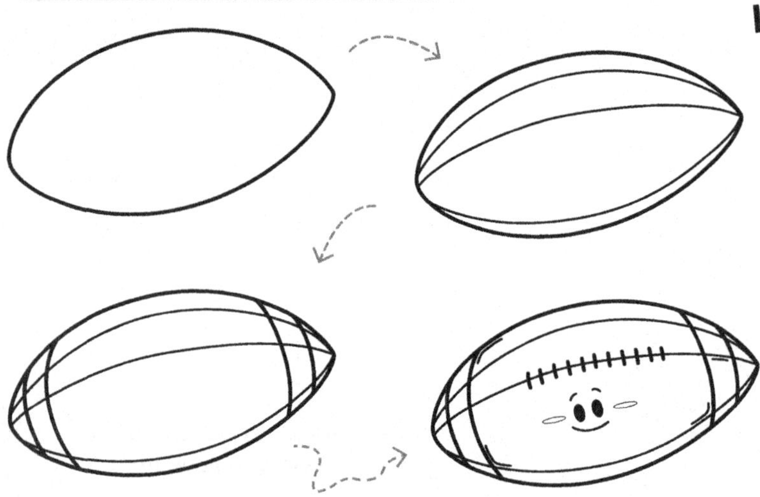

It's your turn!

Don't be afraid to try new things, mix colors and have fun!

TABLE TENNIS RACKET

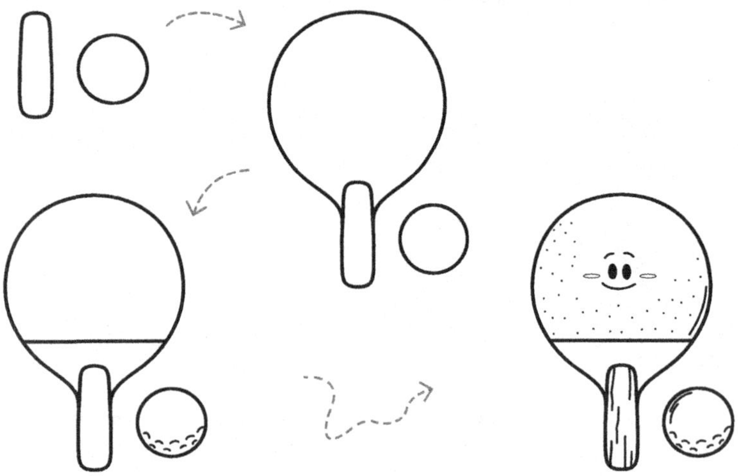

It's your turn!

Don't be afraid to try new things, mix colors and have fun!

BILLIARD BALL

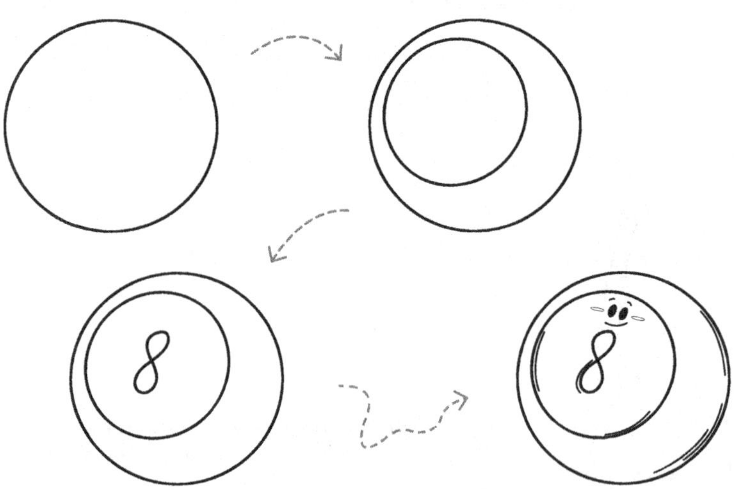

It's your turn!

Don't be afraid to try new things, mix colors and have fun!

SKI

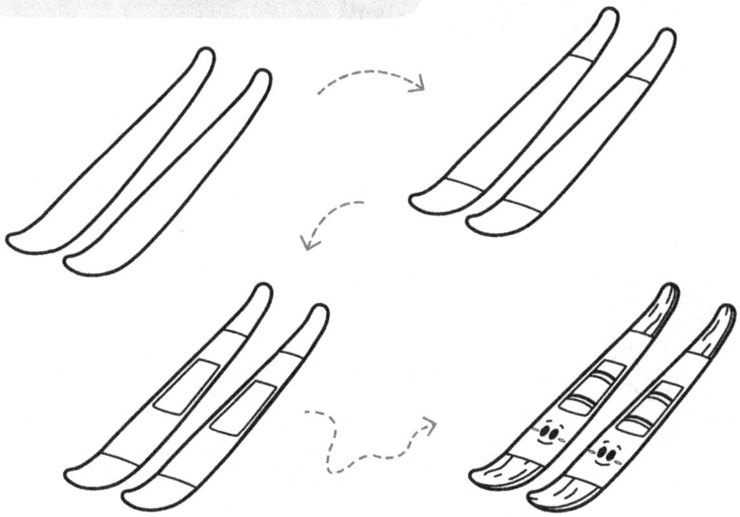

It's your turn!

Don't be afraid to try new things, mix colors and have fun!

BIKING GLOVE

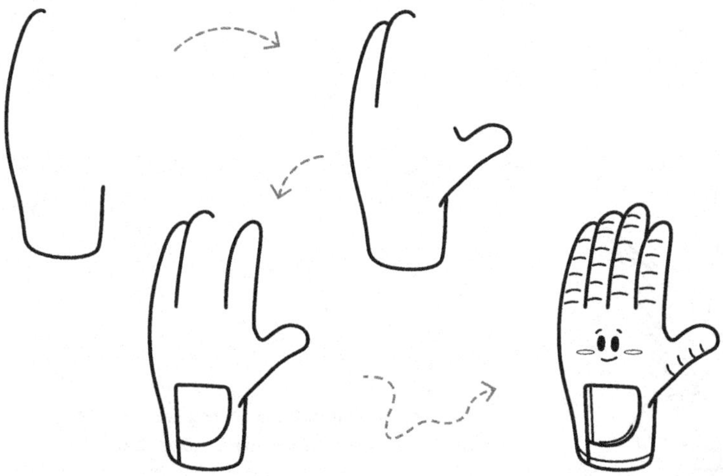

It's your turn!

Don't be afraid to try new things, mix colors and have fun!

ROLLERBLADES

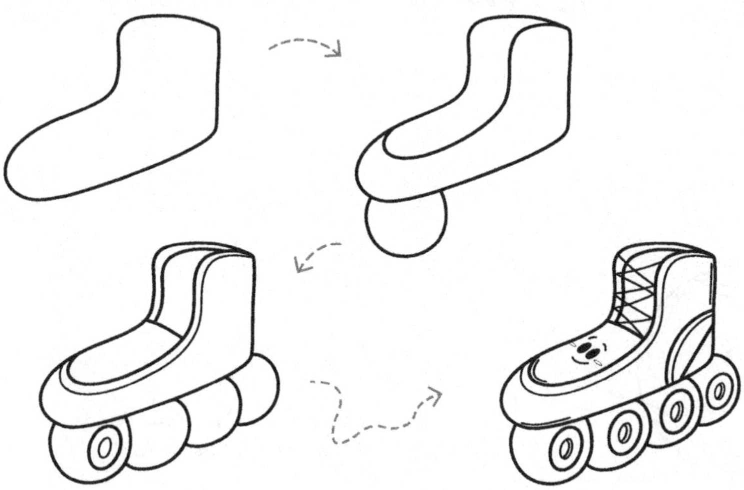

It's your turn!

Don't be afraid to try new things, mix colors and have fun!

ARCHERY TARGET

It's your turn!

Don't be afraid to try new things, mix colors and have fun!

CHINESE HACKY SACK

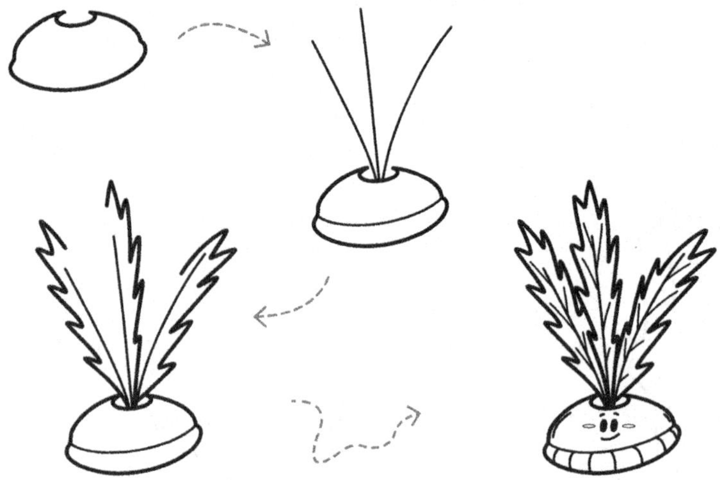

It's your turn!

Don't be afraid to try new things, mix colors and have fun!

BOWLING BALL

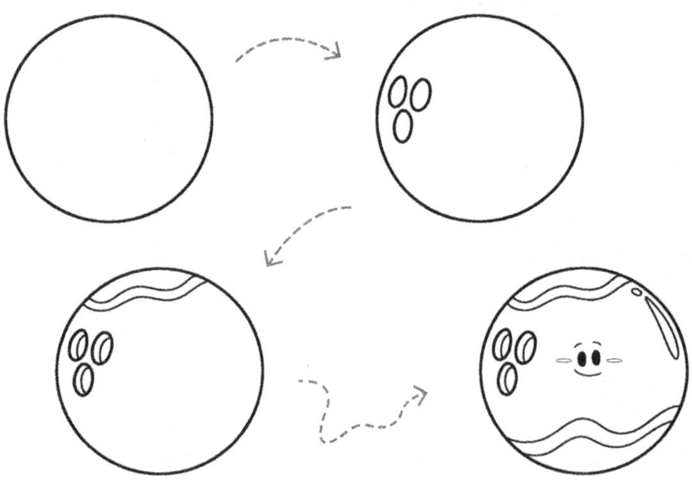

It's your turn!

Don't be afraid to try new things, mix colors and have fun!

TENNIS RACKET

It's your turn!

Don't be afraid to try new things, mix colors and have fun!

SCUBA OXYGEN TANKS

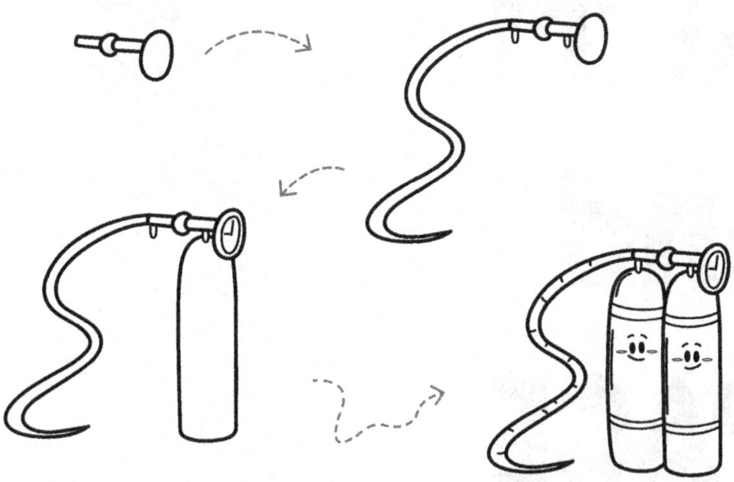

It's your turn!

Don't be afraid to try new things, mix colors and have fun!

SCI-FI and SPACE

Blast off to the stars! From alien ships to battle robots and cosmic creatures, this chapter is filled with out-of-this-world fun.

ALIEN SPACESHIP

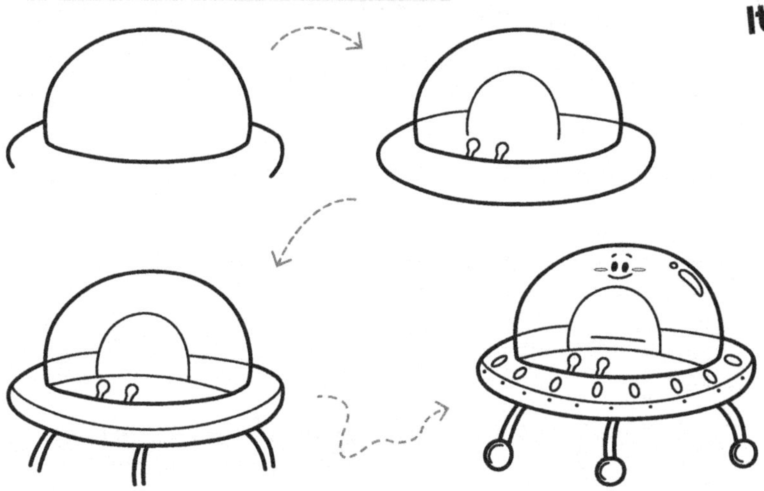

It's your turn!

Don't be afraid to try new things, mix colors and have fun!

NET WITH STARS

It's your turn!

Don't be afraid to try new things, mix colors and have fun!

ASTRONAUT FLOATING

It's your turn!

Don't be afraid to try new things, mix colors and have fun!

MOON BASE

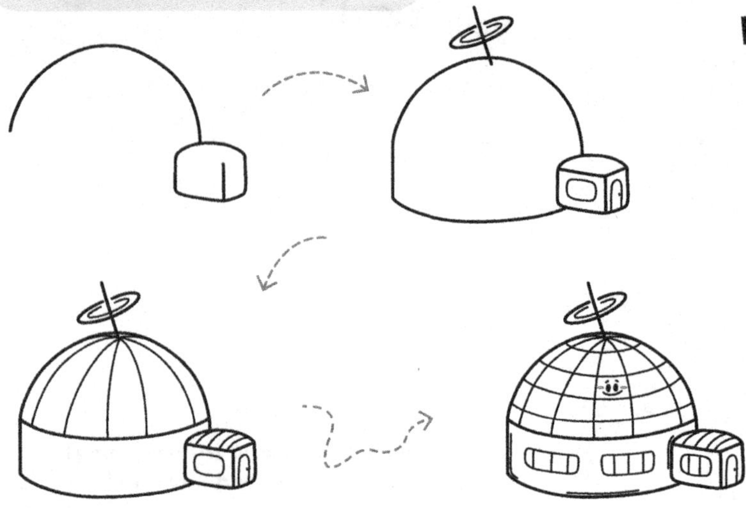

It's your turn!

Don't be afraid to try new things, mix colors and have fun!

STAR CLUSTER

It's your turn!

Don't be afraid to try new things, mix colors and have fun!

BLACK HOLE

It's your turn!

Don't be afraid to try new things, mix colors and have fun!

SPACE TELESCOPE

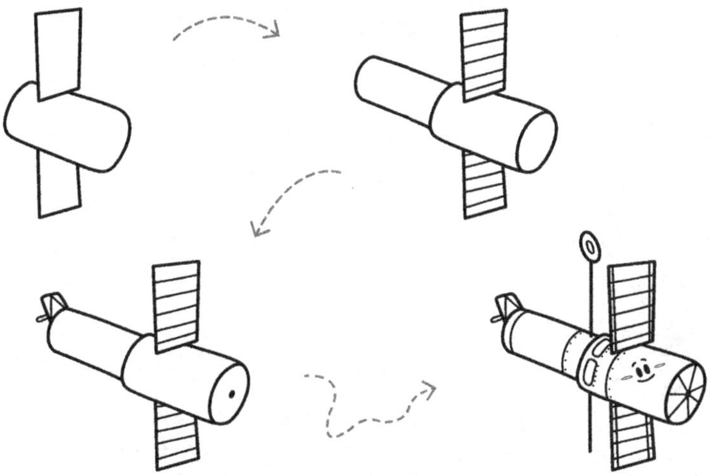

It's your turn!

Don't be afraid to try new things, mix colors and have fun!

FUTURISTIC PLANET

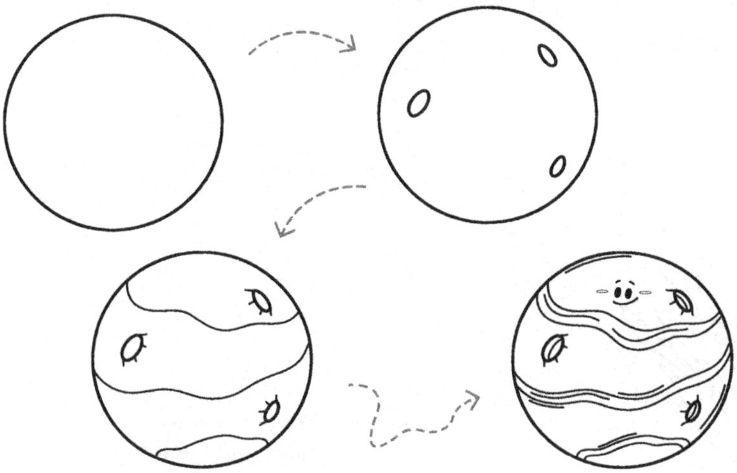

It's your turn!

Don't be afraid to try new things, mix colors and have fun!

ATOM

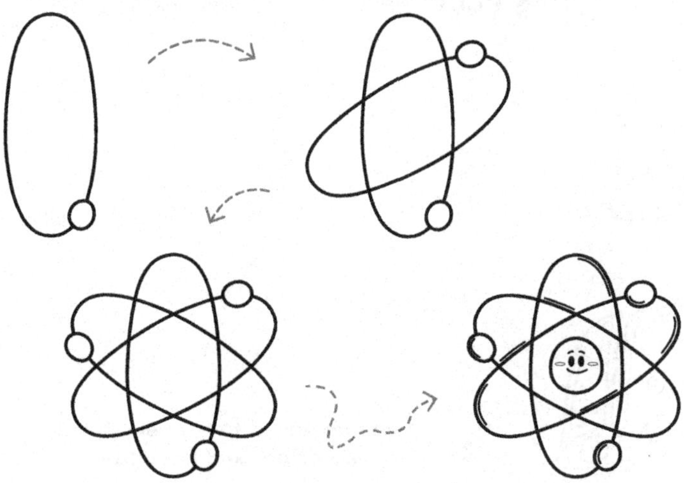

It's your turn!

Don't be afraid to try new things, mix colors and have fun!

SUPERNOVA EXPLOSION

It's your turn!

Don't be afraid to try new things, mix colors and have fun!

METEOR

It's your turn!

Don't be afraid to try new things, mix colors and have fun!

SPACESHIP COCKPIT

It's your turn!

Don't be afraid to try new things, mix colors and have fun!

PLANET EARTH

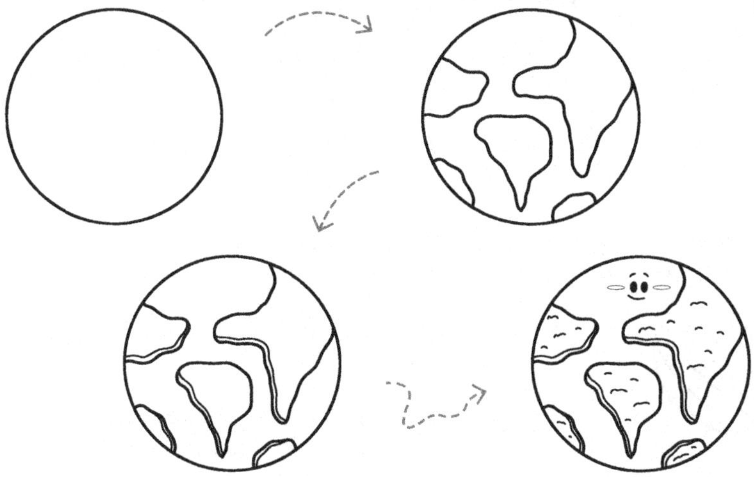

It's your turn!

Don't be afraid to try new things, mix colors and have fun!

ROBOT ASSISTANT

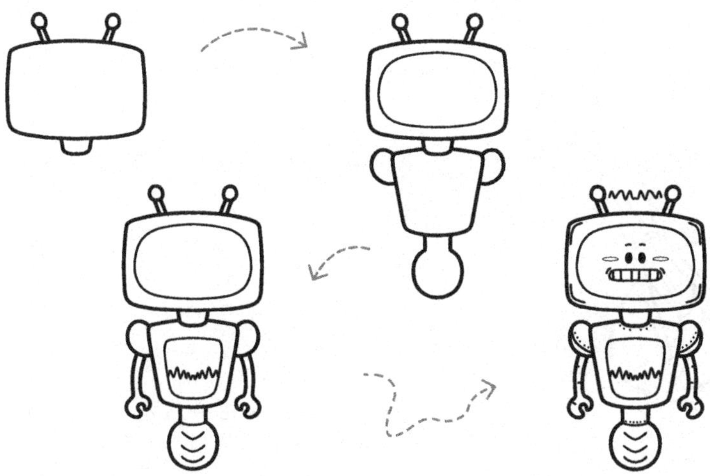

It's your turn!

Don't be afraid to try new things, mix colors and have fun!

ALIEN RADIO

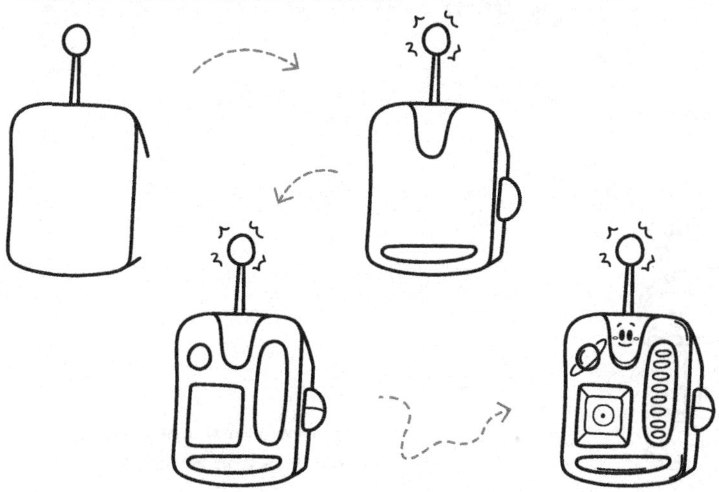

It's your turn!

Don't be afraid to try new things, mix colors and have fun!

SATURN

It's your turn!

Don't be afraid to try new things, mix colors and have fun!

SATELLITE DISH

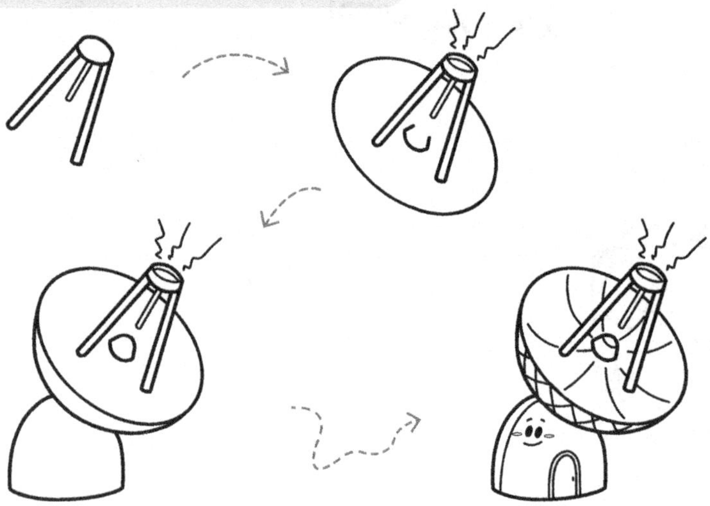

It's your turn!

Don't be afraid to try new things, mix colors and have fun!

WHEELED ROBOT

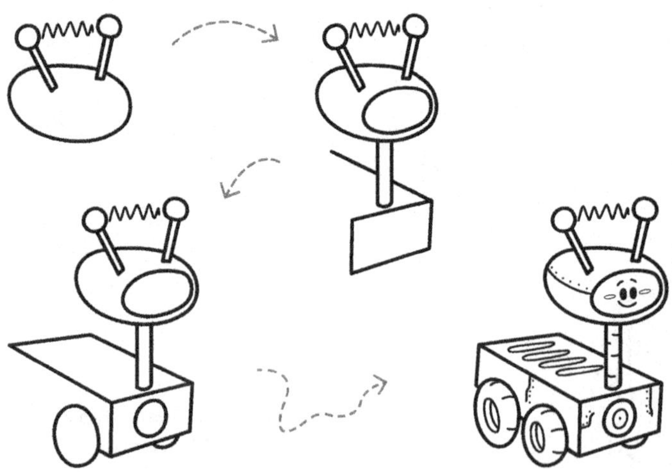

It's your turn!

Don't be afraid to try new things, mix colors and have fun!

SPACE DOCKING STATION

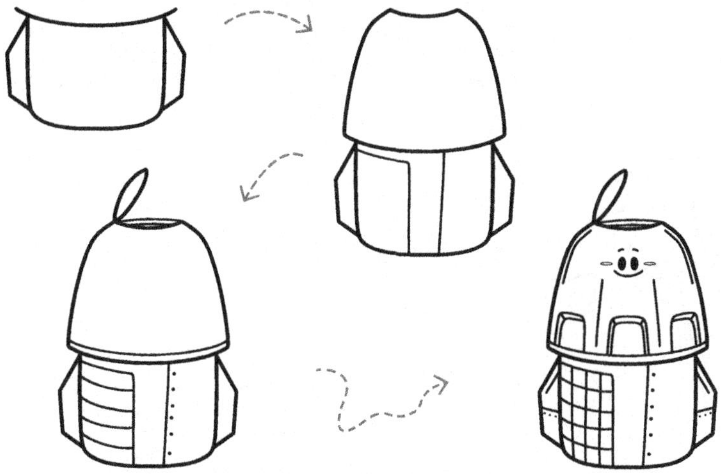

It's your turn!

Don't be afraid to try new things, mix colors and have fun!

SOLAR SYSTEM RINGS

It's your turn!

Don't be afraid to try new things, mix colors and have fun!

COOL OBJECTS and FUN STUFF

Ready for random coolness? Draw awesome gadgets, adventure gear, and fun surprises you didn't even know you wanted to sketch!

TREASURE CHEST

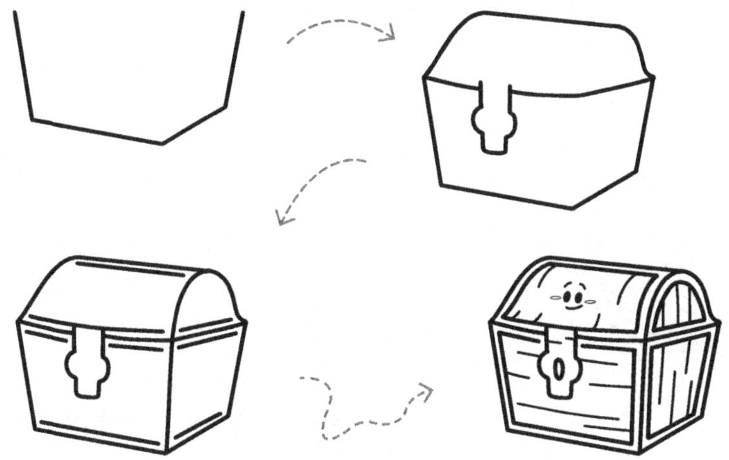

It's your turn!

Don't be afraid to try new things,
mix colors and have fun!

TREASURE MAP

It's your turn!

Don't be afraid to try new things,
mix colors and have fun!

RACING TROPHY

It's your turn!

Don't be afraid to try new things,
mix colors and have fun!

MAGNIFYING GLASS

It's your turn!

Don't be afraid to try new things, mix colors and have fun!

TIME PORTAL

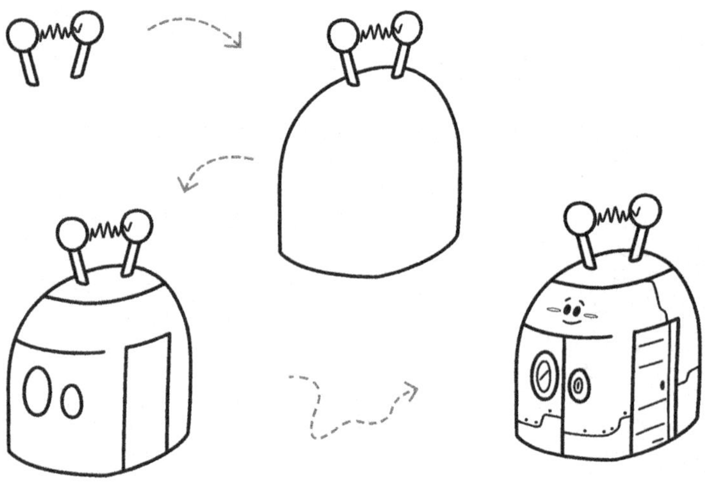

It's your turn!

Don't be afraid to try new things, mix colors and have fun!

MAGIC PORTAL

It's your turn!

Don't be afraid to try new things, mix colors and have fun!

HAMMER

It's your turn!

Don't be afraid to try new things, mix colors and have fun!

GAME CONTROLLER

It's your turn!

Don't be afraid to try new things, mix colors and have fun!

HAND HOLDING FIREBALL

It's your turn!

Don't be afraid to try new things, mix colors and have fun!

EXPLOSION

It's your turn!

Don't be afraid to try new things, mix colors and have fun!

COMIC POW!

It's your turn!

Don't be afraid to try new things, mix colors and have fun!

MICROPHONE

It's your turn!

Don't be afraid to try new things, mix colors and have fun!

DIGITAL MONSTER PET

It's your turn!

Don't be afraid to try new things, mix colors and have fun!

GRAFFITI ART

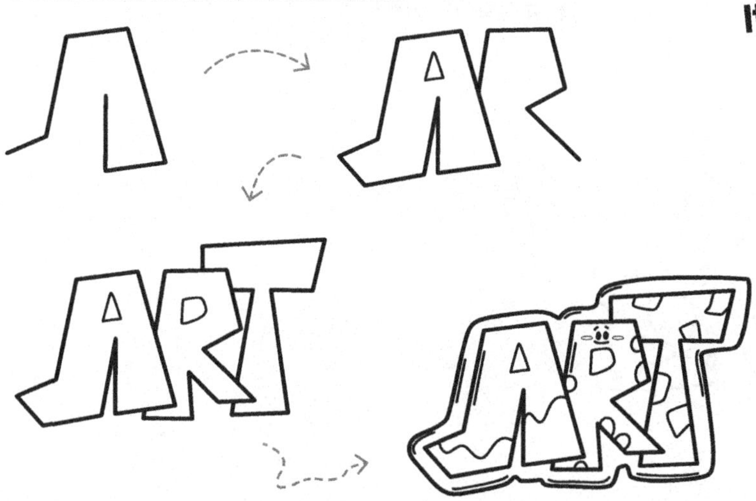

It's your turn!

Don't be afraid to try new things, mix colors and have fun!

SECRET CAVE ENTRANCE

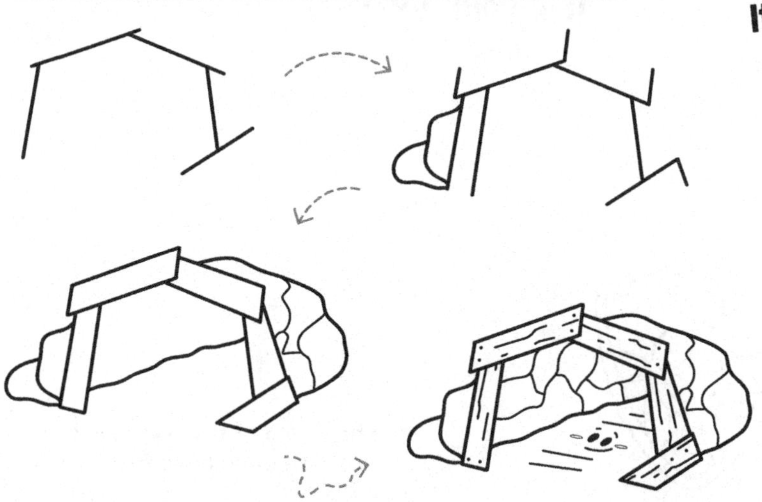

It's your turn!

Don't be afraid to try new things, mix colors and have fun!

CAVEMAN

It's your turn!

Don't be afraid to try new things, mix colors and have fun!

PIRATE FLAG

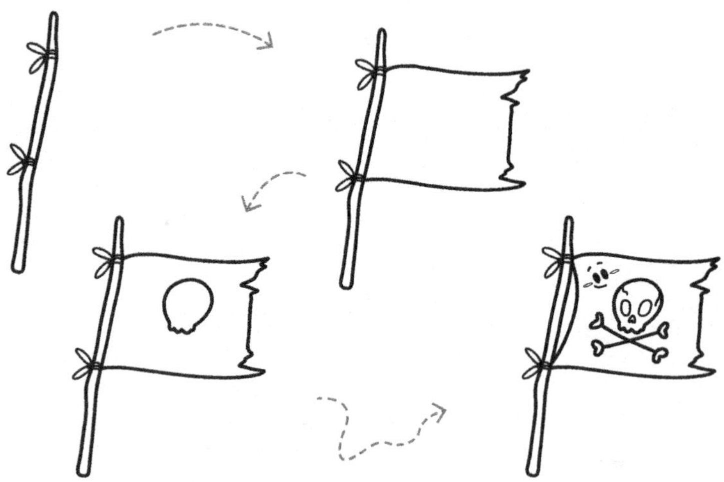

It's your turn!

Don't be afraid to try new things, mix colors and have fun!

MEDIEVAL SHIELD

It's your turn!

Don't be afraid to try new things, mix colors and have fun!

MAD SCIENTIST

It's your turn!

Don't be afraid to try new things, mix colors and have fun!

SPY EARBUD

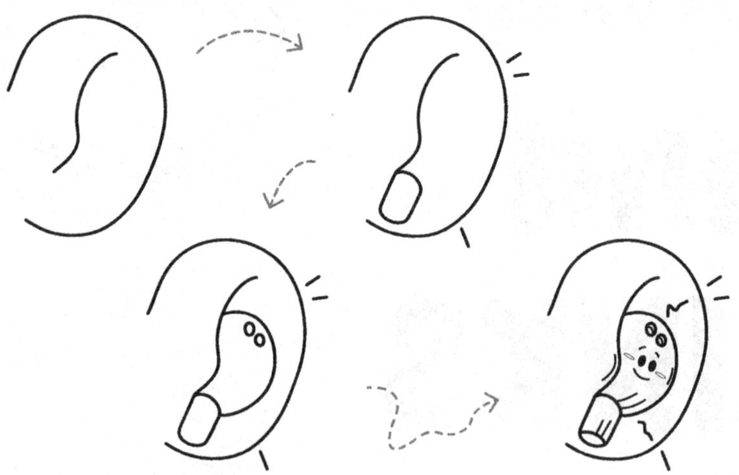

It's your turn!

Don't be afraid to try new things, mix colors and have fun!

FOOD and DRINKS

Feeling hungry? Draw mouthwatering snacks, refreshing drinks, and tasty treats that are as cool to draw as they are to eat.

PIZZA SLICE

It's your turn!

Don't be afraid to try new things, mix colors and have fun!

HAMBURGER

It's your turn!

Don't be afraid to try new things, mix colors and have fun!

HOT DOG

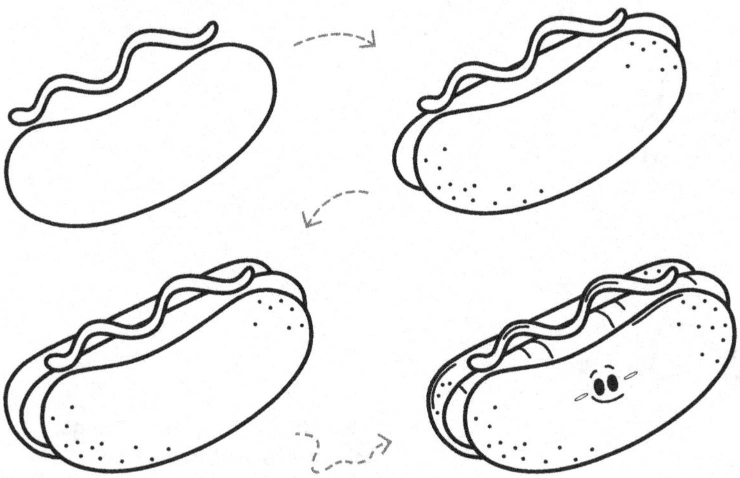

It's your turn!

Don't be afraid to try new things, mix colors and have fun!

FRENCH FRIES

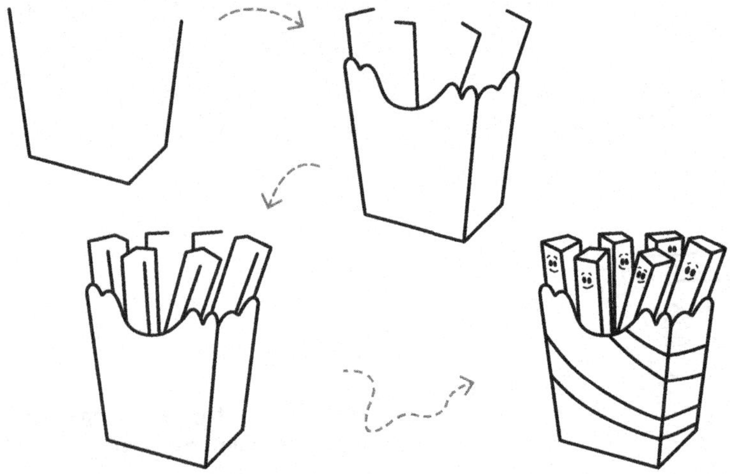

It's your turn!

Don't be afraid to try new things, mix colors and have fun!

CHICKEN NUGGETS

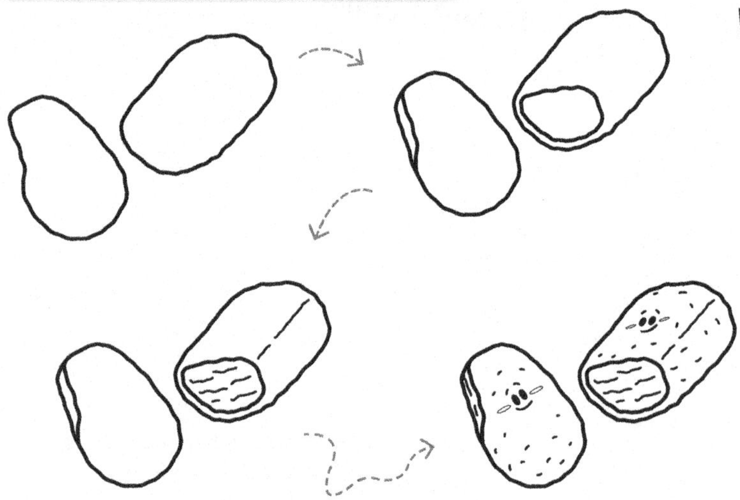

It's your turn!

Don't be afraid to try new things, mix colors and have fun!

SPAGHETTI WITH MEATBALLS

It's your turn!

Don't be afraid to try new things, mix colors and have fun!

TACOS

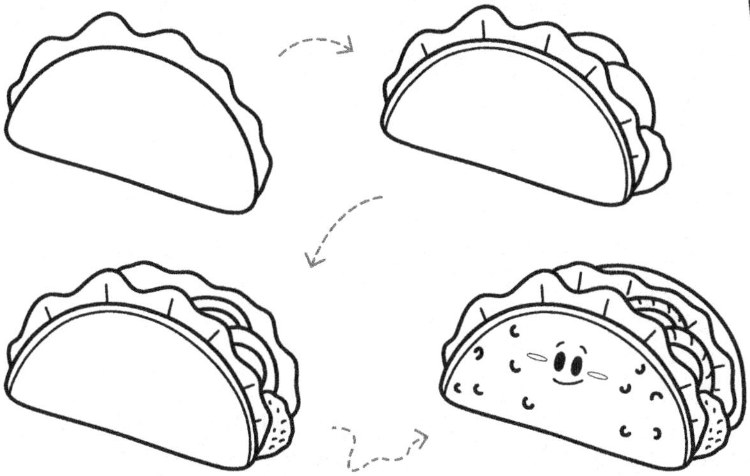

It's your turn!

Don't be afraid to try new things,
mix colors and have fun!

SUSHI ROLL

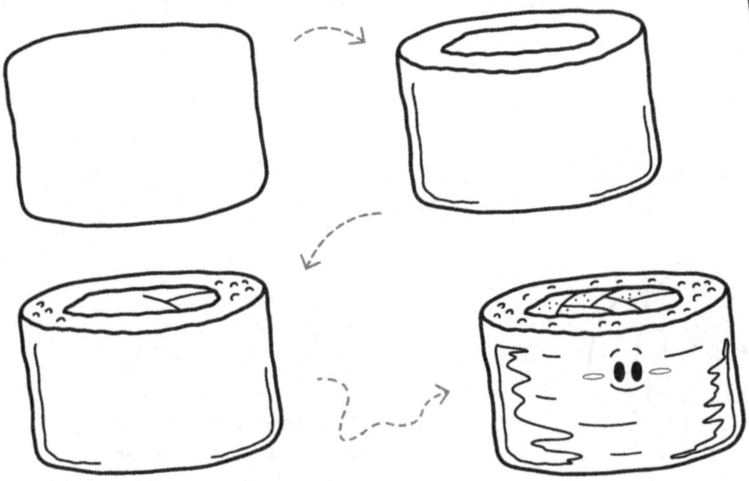

It's your turn!

Don't be afraid to try new things,
mix colors and have fun!

BBQ RIBS

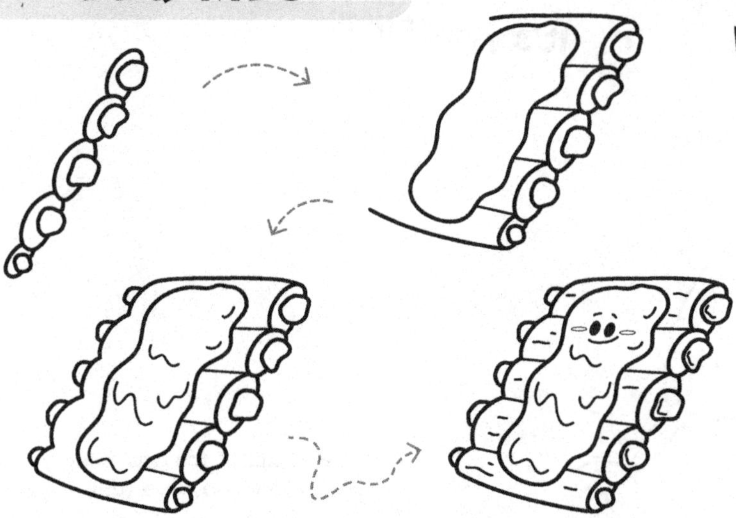

It's your turn!

Don't be afraid to try new things,
mix colors and have fun!

NACHOS

It's your turn!

Don't be afraid to try new things, mix colors and have fun!

STEAK WITH GRILL MARKS

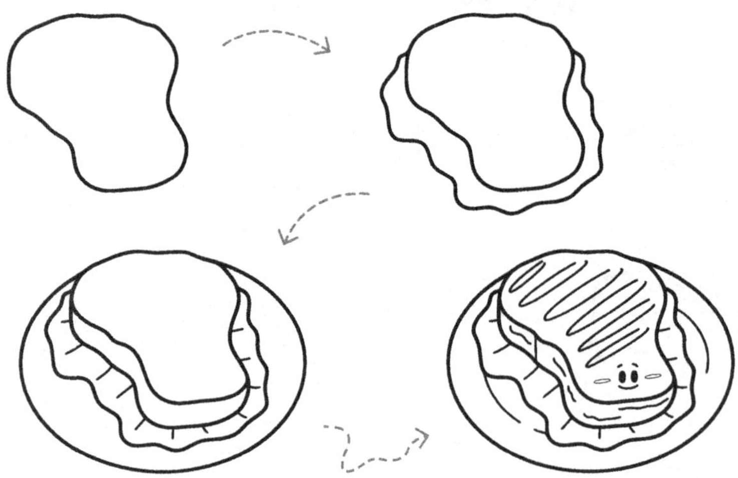

It's your turn!

Don't be afraid to try new things, mix colors and have fun!

FRIED CHICKEN DRUMSTICK

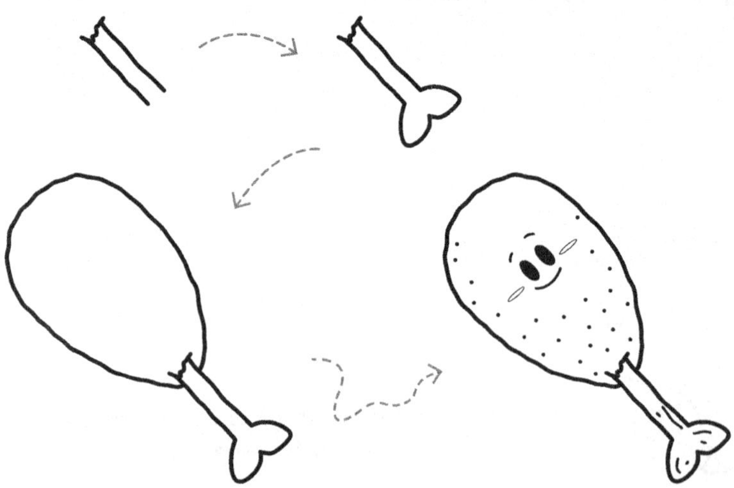

It's your turn!

Don't be afraid to try new things, mix colors and have fun!

MAC AND CHEESE BOWL

It's your turn!

Don't be afraid to try new things, mix colors and have fun!

POPCORN BUCKET

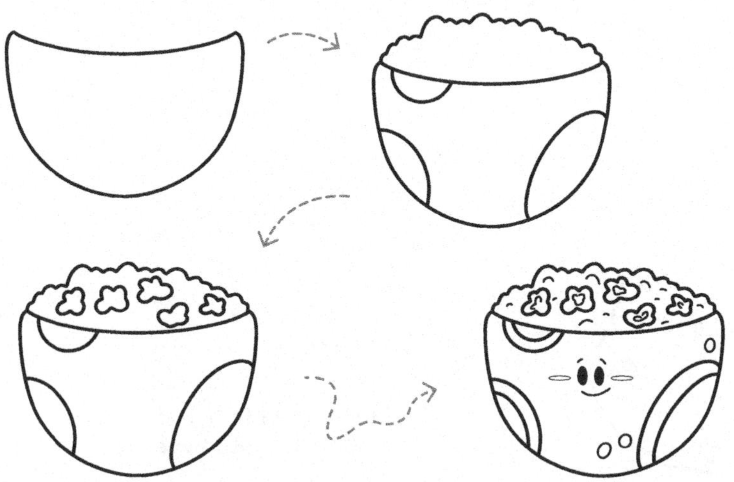

It's your turn!

Don't be afraid to try new things, mix colors and have fun!

CUPCAKE WITH SPRINKLES

It's your turn!

Don't be afraid to try new things, mix colors and have fun!

ICE CREAM CONE

It's your turn!

Don't be afraid to try new things,
mix colors and have fun!

CHOCOLATE CHIP COOKIE

It's your turn!

Don't be afraid to try new things,
mix colors and have fun!

DOUGHNUT WITH SPRINKLES

It's your turn!

Don't be afraid to try new things,
mix colors and have fun!

CUPCAKE WITH CHERRY ON TOP

It's your turn!

Don't be afraid to try new things, mix colors and have fun!

BROWNIE SQUARE

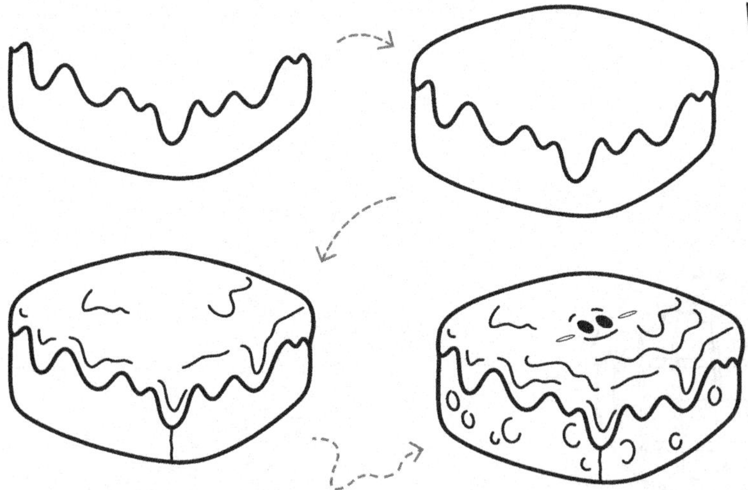

It's your turn!

Don't be afraid to try new things, mix colors and have fun!

COTTON CANDY STICK

It's your turn!

Don't be afraid to try new things, mix colors and have fun!

APPLE PIE SLICE

It's your turn!

Don't be afraid to try new things, mix colors and have fun!

WAFFLE WITH SYRUP

It's your turn!

Don't be afraid to try new things, mix colors and have fun!

BIRTHDAY CAKE

It's your turn!

Don't be afraid to try new things, mix colors and have fun!

JELLY BEANS

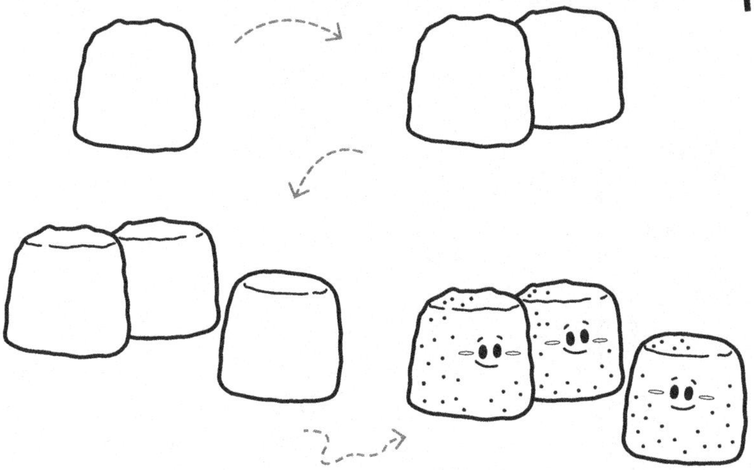

It's your turn!

Don't be afraid to try new things, mix colors and have fun!

MILKSHAKE WITH WHIPPED CREAM

It's your turn!

Don't be afraid to try new things, mix colors and have fun!

FIZZY SODA CAN

It's your turn!

Don't be afraid to try new things, mix colors and have fun!

SPORTS ENERGY DRINK

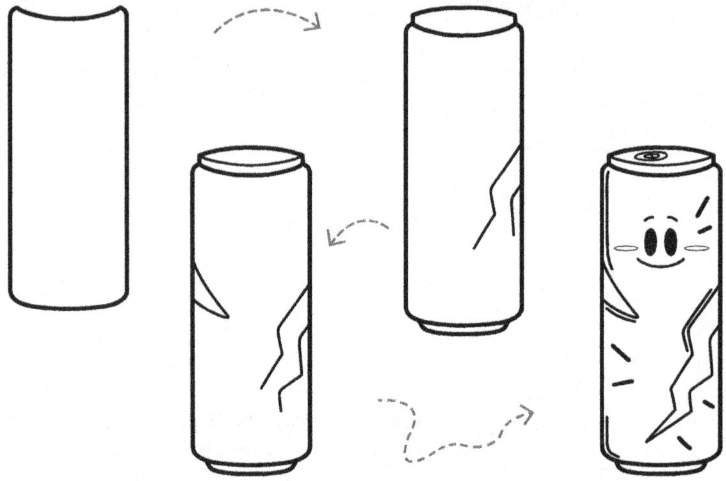

It's your turn!

Don't be afraid to try new things, mix colors and have fun!

LEMONADE WITH ICE CUBES

It's your turn!

Don't be afraid to try new things, mix colors and have fun!

DRINK IN A GLASS

It's your turn!

Don't be afraid to try new things, mix colors and have fun!

HOLIDAY and FESTIVE CHARACTERS

Time to celebrate! Draw fun holiday characters, festive decorations, and party-ready designs perfect for any season.

SANTA CLAUS

It's your turn!

Don't be afraid to try new things, mix colors and have fun!

CHRISTMAS TREE WITH ORNAMENTS

It's your turn!

Don't be afraid to try new things, mix colors and have fun!

SNOWMAN WITH HAT

It's your turn!

Don't be afraid to try new things, mix colors and have fun!

REINDEER WITH COLLAR

It's your turn!

Don't be afraid to try new things, mix colors and have fun!

GINGERBREAD MAN

It's your turn!

Don't be afraid to try new things, mix colors and have fun!

CHRISTMAS STOCKING WITH GIFTS

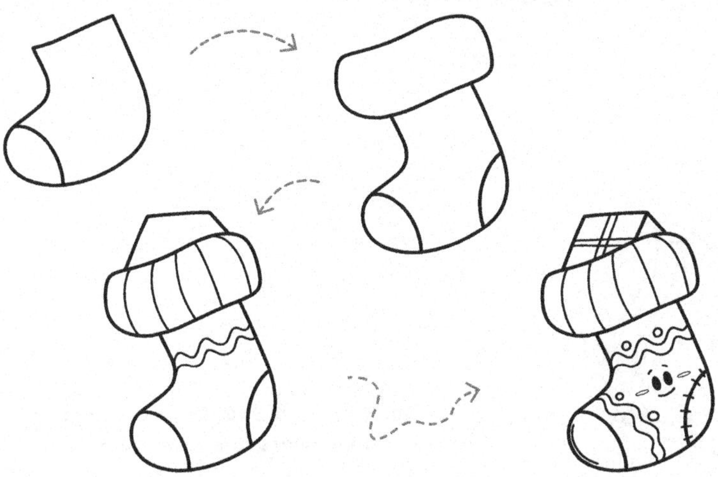

It's your turn!

Don't be afraid to try new things, mix colors and have fun!

ELF

It's your turn!

Don't be afraid to try new things,
mix colors and have fun!

WRAPPED CHRISTMAS PRESENT

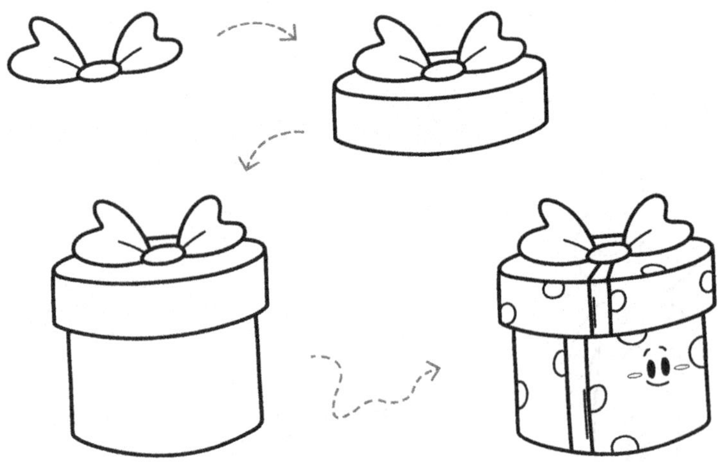

It's your turn!

Don't be afraid to try new things,
mix colors and have fun!

SANTA'S SLEIGH

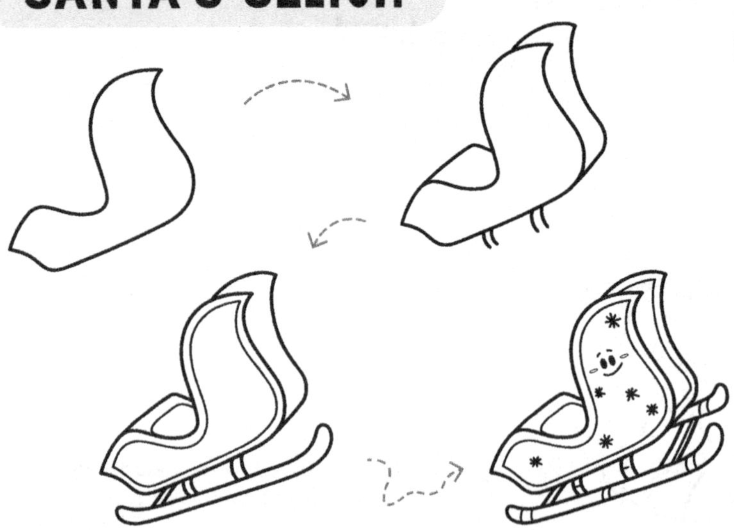

It's your turn!

Don't be afraid to try new things,
mix colors and have fun!

CHRISTMAS FIREPLACE

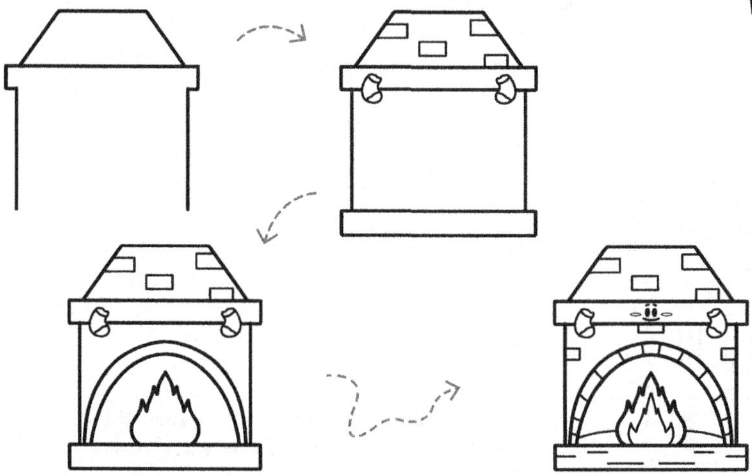

It's your turn!

Don't be afraid to try new things,
mix colors and have fun!

PUMPKIN

It's your turn!

Don't be afraid to try new things,
mix colors and have fun!

SPOOKY GHOST

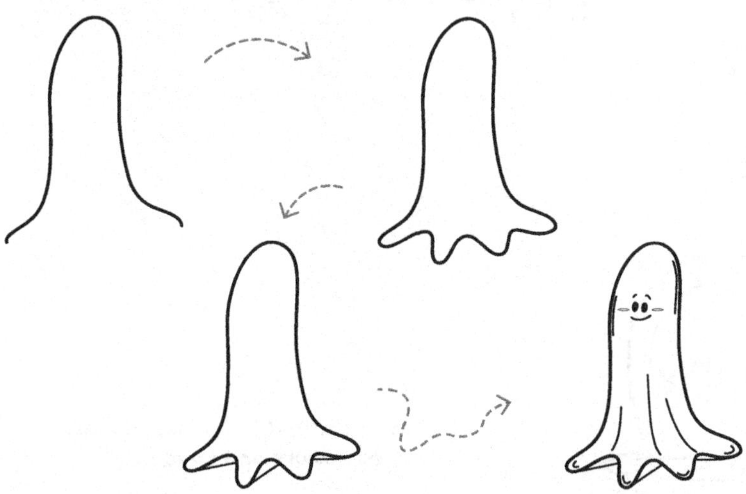

It's your turn!

Don't be afraid to try new things,
mix colors and have fun!

DRACULA VAMPIRE

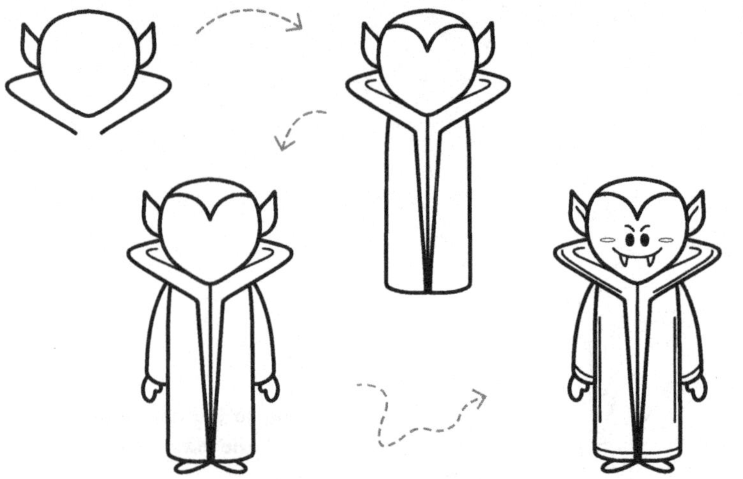

It's your turn!

Don't be afraid to try new things, mix colors and have fun!

FRANKENSTEIN'S MONSTER

It's your turn!

Don't be afraid to try new things, mix colors and have fun!

TOMBSTONE

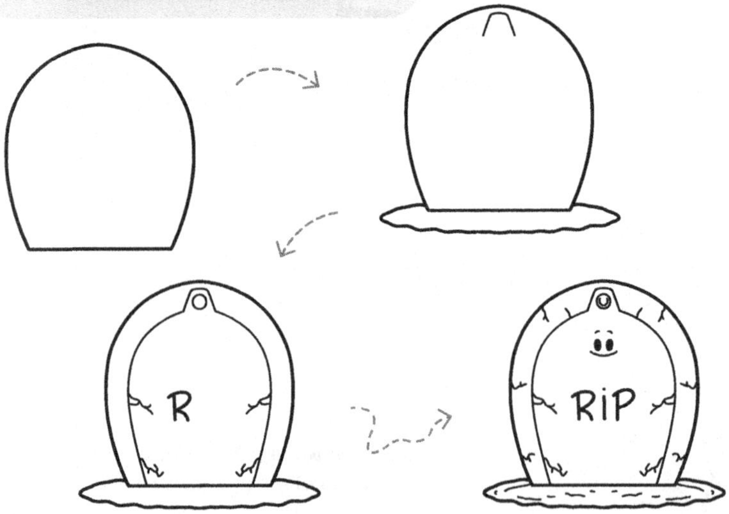

It's your turn!

Don't be afraid to try new things, mix colors and have fun!

HAUNTED HOUSE

It's your turn!

Don't be afraid to try new things, mix colors and have fun!

DANCING SKELETON

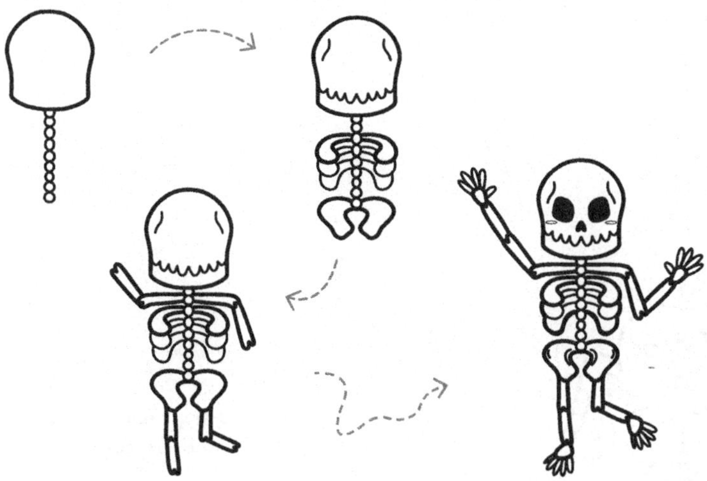

It's your turn!

Don't be afraid to try new things, mix colors and have fun!

WITCH

It's your turn!

Don't be afraid to try new things, mix colors and have fun!

TRICK-OR-TREAT BAG

It's your turn!

Don't be afraid to try new things, mix colors and have fun!

CREEPY SPIDER

It's your turn!

Don't be afraid to try new things, mix colors and have fun!

EASTER BUNNY HOLDING AN EGG

It's your turn!

Don't be afraid to try new things, mix colors and have fun!

EASTER EGG

It's your turn!

Don't be afraid to try new things,
mix colors and have fun!

FIREWORKS FOR NEW YEAR'S EVE

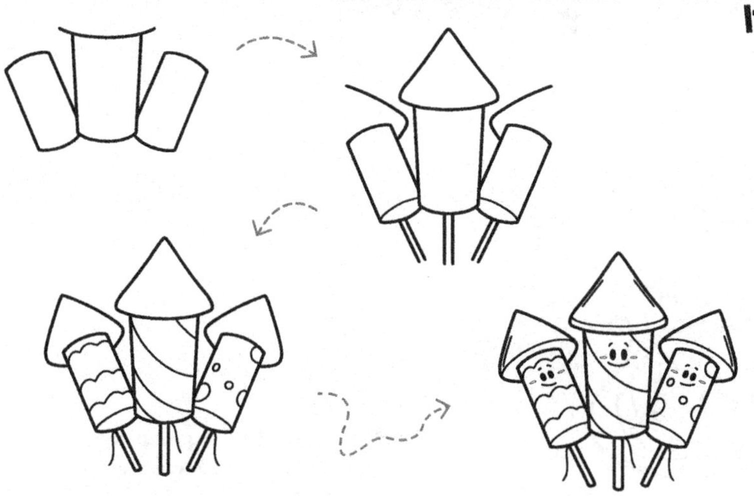

It's your turn!

Don't be afraid to try new things,
mix colors and have fun!

PARTY HAT

It's your turn!

Don't be afraid to try new things,
mix colors and have fun!

BIRTHDAY BALLOONS

It's your turn!

Don't be afraid to try new things, mix colors and have fun!

THANKSGIVING TURKEY

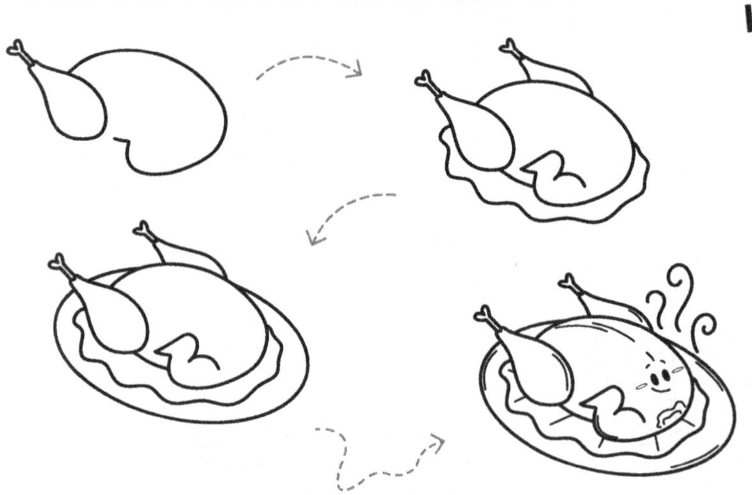

It's your turn!

Don't be afraid to try new things, mix colors and have fun!

SHAMROCK FOR ST. PATRICK'S DAY

It's your turn!

Don't be afraid to try new things, mix colors and have fun!

PIRATE SKULL FOR TALK LIKE A PIRATE DAY

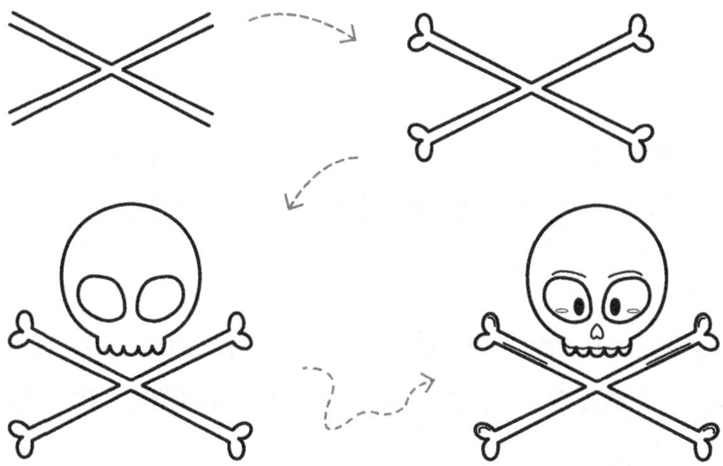

It's your turn!

Don't be afraid to try new things, mix colors and have fun!

PEN

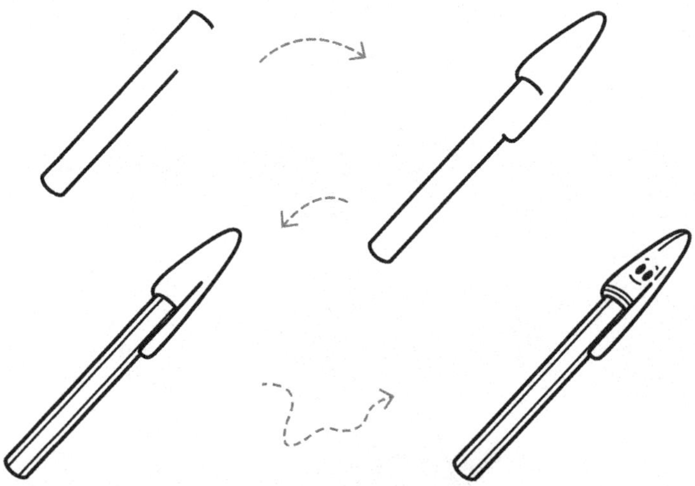

It's your turn!

Don't be afraid to try new things, mix colors and have fun!

IPAD

It's your turn!

Don't be afraid to try new things, mix colors and have fun!

You Did It — Way to Go, Artist!

Look at everything you've drawn! From speedy race cars to fire-breathing dragons, you've filled these pages with action-packed, awesome drawings—and you did an amazing job.

Now you can use your new skills to create cool doodles on notebooks, cards, posters, or anywhere you like. You can even surprise your friends and family with your art as special handmade gifts!

There's no limit to what you can draw next. Keep practicing, stay creative, and explore more exciting adventures with our other how-to-draw books.

Stay awesome, and keep drawing!

Made in United States
Orlando, FL
23 December 2025

75089779R00070